.....The Attack on Pearl Harbor

Japanese Plane Attack Routes

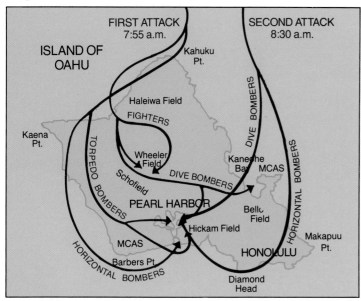

Launched in two separate attacks, 353 planes wove a complicated pattern that proved the skill of the Japanese pilots.

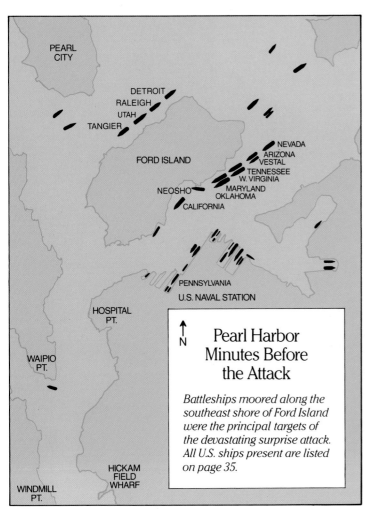

Pearl Harbor Minutes Before the Attack

Battleships moored along the southeast shore of Ford Island were the principal targets of the devastating surprise attack. All U.S. ships present are listed on page 35.

There was a short lull in the fury of the attack at about 8:30. At that time the *Nevada,* despite her wounds, managed to get underway and move down the channel toward the open sea. Before the *Nevada* could clear the harbor a second wave of 170 Japanese planes, launched 30 minutes after the first, appeared over the harbor. They concentrated their attacks on the moving battleship, hoping to sink her in the channel and block the narrow entrance to Pearl Harbor. On orders from the harbor control tower the *Nevada* beached herself at Hospital Point and the channel remained clear.

When the attack ended shortly before 10:00 am, less than two hours after it had begun, the American forces had paid a fearful price. Twenty-one ships of the U.S. Pacific Fleet were sunk or damaged: the battleships *Arizona, Nevada, Tennessee, Maryland, Oklahoma, West Virginia, California* and *Pennsylvania;* the cruisers *Raleigh, Helena* and *Honolulu;* the destroyers *Downes, Cassin, Shaw* and *Helm;* the seaplane tender *Curtiss;* the target ship (ex-battleship) *Utah;* the repair ship *Vestal;* the minelayer *Oglala;* the tug *Sotoyomo;* and Floating Drydock Number 2. Aircraft losses were 188 destroyed and 159 damaged—the great majority hit before they had a chance to take off. American dead numbered 2,403. That figure included 68 civilian dead, most of them killed by improperly fused antiaircraft shells landing in Honolulu. There were 1,178 military and civilian wounded.

Japanese losses were comparatively light. Twenty-nine planes, less than 10% of the attacking force, failed to return to their carriers.

The Japanese success was overwhelming, but it was not complete. They failed to damage any American aircraft carriers, which by a stroke of luck, had been absent from the harbor. They neglected to damage the shoreside facilities at the Pearl Harbor naval base, which played an important role in the Allied victory in World War II. American technological skill raised and repaired all but three* of the ships sunk or damaged at Pearl Harbor. Most importantly, the shock and anger caused by the surprise attack on Pearl Harbor united a divided nation and was translated into a wholehearted commitment to victory in World War II.

Today the USS *Arizona* stands as a reminder of the events of that Sunday morning. It has different meanings for the millions who visit here. But to all of them it speaks silently but eloquently of the distance yet to be travelled before the world lives in peace.

*The *Arizona* and *Oklahoma* were too badly damaged to be salvaged. The obsolete *Utah* was also considered not to be worth the effort.

Remembering Pearl Harbor

The Story of the USS Arizona Memorial

by Michael Slackman
National Park Service

Published by the
Arizona Memorial
Museum Association
Honolulu, Hawaii

SEQUOIA
COMMUNICATIONS

Produced for the Arizona Memorial Museum Association
Design by Gay Hagen, Ron Rubenstein, S. Chamberlin / Printed in Hong Kong

Library of Congress Catalog Card Number: 84-50998 / ISBN 0-917859-18-9

Names of the Arizona's 1,177 dead are engraved in a white marble wall in the Memorial's shrine room.

For My Parents

Acknowledgments

This study would have been impossible without the support and assistance of many people. For their indispensable help I thank: the directors of the *Arizona* Memorial Museum Association for financial support; the association's business manager, Gary Beito; Superintendent Gary Cummins and Chief Ranger John Martini of the National Park Service's USS *Arizona* Memorial for their support and encouragement; Edwin Bearss, Chief Historian, and Gordon Chappell, Western Regional Historian of the National Park Service, for their editorial suggestions; Susan Shaner of the Hawaii State Archives; R.H. "Rock" Rothrock of the Pearl Harbor Naval Base Public Affairs Office; Bill Loo of OICC Mid-Pacific at Pearl Harbor; Gary Barbano of the Pacific Area Office of the National Park Service; Robert Nolan, National Executive Secretary of the Fleet Reserve Association; Victoria Custer, former Executive Secretary of the Pacific War Memorial Association; June Gutmanis, my editor; Don Ackland of Sequoia; and E. Raymond Lewis, Librarian of the House of Representatives.

The following people provided me with recollections of events covered in this study: Robert Barrel, retired director of the Pacific Area Office of the National Park Service; Gary Beito, former business manager of the *Arizona* Memorial Museum Foundation; C.E. Burns, Chief Boatswain's Mate, USN (ret.); George Chaplin, Editor-in-Chief of the Honolulu *Advertiser;* U.S. Marshal and former Hawaii State Representative Faith Evans; H. Tucker Gratz, former Chairman of the Pacific War Memorial Commission; Senator Daniel Inouye; Senator Spark Matsunaga; the late Hawaii State Senator David McClung, who shared not only his recollections, but his files; and Alfred Preis, architect of the USS *Arizona* Memorial. I am grateful to them for sharing their experiences and their time. I am solely responsible for any errors of fact or interpretation.

Finally, I would like to state for the record that I have been employed at various times in the past by several agencies and organizations mentioned in this study: the National Park Service, the *Arizona* Memorial Museum Association (successor organization to the *Arizona* Memorial Museum Foundation), the Hawaii State Legislature, and the Pearl Harbor Memorial Museum.

Front Cover Photo: *"Day of Infamy" oil on canvas by Kipp Soldwedel. Photo by Ship Lore Ltd.*

Back Cover Photo: *Ship's bell from the USS Arizona. Photo by Paul Henning.*

Left: *The Arizona Memorial framed by a Pearl Harbor rainbow. Photo by Allan Seiden.*

Contents

Left: *Salvaged from the floor of Pearl Harbor and weighing 19,585 lbs, one of the Arizona's anchors rests at the Visitor Center entrance.* Photo by: *Paul Henning*

Preface

"A Story of Persistence and Hard Work"

The story of the USS *Arizona* Memorial and Visitor Center is a story of persistence and hard work. Because it involved hundreds of people and spanned more than three decades, it necessarily includes conflict, confusion, and setbacks.

This account does not ignore or minimize those aspects. They comprise part of the historical record. They are included out of respect for the whole truth and to give an objective account of the USS *Arizona* Memorial and Visitor Center.

I have tried to deal with those factors in a spirit of appreciation for the vision, dedication, and goodwill required to overcome the obstacles in the path of all who worked to establish the Memorial and the Visitor Center.

In writing history it is inevitable that some names appear more often than others. It is not my purpose to exaggerate or denigrate the work of any individual, group or agency, but to reflect the facts recorded in available sources. Everyone mentioned in this account—and many more who are not—contributed to the achievement of a common goal. One of those individuals expressed it best when he said, "Nobody was more important than everybody."

Left: *News of the Pearl Harbor attack made headlines throughout the world. Sailors raising the Stars and Stripes above the Arizona's wreckage made the cover of LIFE Magazine 15 years after the attack.*

Below: *Many Pearl Harbor dead are buried in National Memorial Cemetery of the Pacific —also called Punchbowl National Cemetery because of its location in Punchbowl Crater, an extinct volcanic feature.*

Part I: Before the Attack

Historic Pearl Harbor

Pearl Harbor, known to the ancient Hawaiians as Puuloa, was an important source of food before Westerners arrived in Hawaii. Its many fish ponds provided sustenance to the people of the surrounding area. Pearl Harbor acquired its modern name from the pearl oysters found there until the late 19th century. It was also the legendary home of the shark goddess Ka'ahupahau.

The harbor first came to the attention of Europeans in the 1790s when Captain George Vancouver discovered the entrance to Pearl Harbor. Many 19th century visitors to Hawaii noted that the sheltered waters of Pearl Harbor offered an ideal naval anchorage.

In 1872 the United States government dispatched Lieutenant General John MacAllister Schofield to Hawaii to assess the islands' strategic value. Schofield recognized the potential of Pearl Harbor and recommended that the U.S. negotiate with the Hawaiian Kingdom for the use of Pearl Harbor. In 1884 the United States and Hawaii signed a treaty which gave the U.S. exclusive rights to establish and maintain a coaling and repair station at Pearl Harbor in exchange for duty-free entry of Hawaiian sugar into the American market.

Until 1900 coaling was done at a station at Honolulu which consisted of a dilapidated shed on rented ground with a capacity of 1,000 tons. In that year two piers were constructed, two slips excavated, and the first dredging of Pearl Harbor began. The following year, the U.S. began purchasing lands around the harbor under eminent domain proceedings. In 1909 construction of a drydock began, but disaster struck in 1913 when the concrete foundation for the new drydock collapsed. On the advice of the project's Hawaiian workers a kahuna, or Hawaiian priest, was retained to appease Ka'ahupahau, Pearl Harbor's shark goddess. The drydock was completed without further incident in 1919.

By 1941 Pearl Harbor was the headquarters of the U.S. Pacific Fleet. It remains today one of the largest naval bases in the world and an important center of American military power.

Left: *Painted three years before the attack, Arthur Beaumont's "Cease Present Exercise" shows the USS Arizona and the USS New Mexico leading the fleet.*

Below: *By 1920, a rail line connected Honolulu and Pearl Harbor.*

Ford Island looking northeast 15 years before the war. Photograph by the Bureau of Aeronautics.

Pearl Harbor from Aiea Heights on a peaceful day shortly before World War II.

In 1934, Pearl Harbor's main entrance was little more than a gate across a two lane road.

Dredging the Pearl Harbor channel, 1911.

In this 1927 view, Pearl Harbor was a quiet backdrop for the Honolulu Plantation Co. sugar mill.

The Arizona and the Pacific Fleet in full glory seen from the same vantage point less than 10 years later.

The USS Arizona, Ship of Destiny

Early in the twentieth century the battleship was in many ways the ultimate weapon of the era. Every nation with pretensions to great power status had a fleet of these fearsome warships. They were designed to project national power over the oceans of the world, defend the nation's commercial and political interests in distant lands, and overawe potential enemies.

The Navy accepted the design for the USS *Arizona* in 1913, and Congress authorized construction the same year. The *Arizona*'s keel was laid down at the Brooklyn Navy Yard in 1914. The following year the ship was launched and christened by Miss Esther Ross, daughter of one of Arizona's pioneer families. The ship was commissioned in 1917 after her construction was completed at a cost of nearly $13,000,000.

When the *Arizona* was completed she was one of the world's most powerful warships. With a standard displacement of more than 31,000 tons, she measured 608 feet long and 97 feet at maximum beam.

Her main armament consisted of twelve 14-inch guns in four turrets (two forward, two aft) mounting three guns apiece. Each gun fired a 1,400 pound projectile more than ten miles.

These monster cannon were complemented by a secondary battery of twenty-two 5-inch 51 caliber guns. Sixteen were mounted in casemates amidships and forward on the main deck level, four were casemated aft on the second deck, and the remaining two stood in the open atop the forecastle.

Sailors lining the deck of the Arizona in the 1930s.

The 14 inch guns of the main battery were designed to outrange and sink opposing battleships, while the secondary armament served as protection against torpedo boats and other small craft.

Twelve thousand, five hundred tons of armor—more than a third of the *Arizona's* displacement—protected the ship and crew from enemy gunfire. All vital components were protected by thick armor plating. Thirteen and a half inches of steel girdled the hull at the waterline, and a full foot and a half shielded the turret faceplates.

A crew of more than 1,000 officers and men operated the machinery, manned the guns, and performed the myriad duties incidental to the operation of the vessel. Clerks, musicians, bakers, carpenters and other specialists composed part of the mosaic of life aboard a great warship. Rising more than a hundred feet above the main deck of this floating city were two cage masts, looking from a distance like towers of open weave basketry.

The ship was commissioned during the First World War but fought no battles in that conflict. Instead, the *Arizona* provided gunnery training off the Atlantic Coast. After Germany's surrender she joined the British Grand Fleet for a short time. In 1919 the *Arizona* put in at Smyrna, Turkey, providing an American military presence in that port during the Turkish-Greek war following the collapse of the Ottoman Empire. She rejoined the Atlantic Fleet, serving briefly as fleet flagship in the summer of 1921, before transferring to the Pacific Fleet later that year.

Admiral Isoroku Yamamoto, Commander in Chief of the Japanese Fleet and principal architect of the Pearl Harbor attack. His luck changed six months later at the Midway, and Japan was on the defensive for the rest of the war.

The *Arizona* received a thorough remodelling at the Norfolk Navy Yard in 1929-31. The ship's configuration and appearance changed considerably with the replacement of the cage masts with tripod masts. The hull was modified to an expanded beam of 106 feet, the maximum width allowing passage through the Panama Canal.

The range of the 14 inch guns was increased to nearly twenty miles. The secondary battery configuration was modified considerably. All 5-inch guns were stripped from the forecastle deck, and ten 5-inch 51 caliber guns mounted in the new superstructure deckhouse. There was an additional pair mounted above the deckhouse.

These 51 caliber guns could not be operated effectively against planes, so the deficiency was remedied with the installation of eight 5-inch 25 caliber guns atop the deckhouse. The shorter barreled 25 caliber weapons were especially designed as antiaircraft guns with a high rate of fire and easier maneuverability.

After overhaul the ship operated briefly in the Caribbean, where President Herbert Hoover sailed aboard the *Arizona*. Following that interlude she rejoined the Pacific Fleet, serving as flagship for various battleship divisions, participating in fleet maneuvers, and taking part in Army-Navy maneuvers throughout the 1930s. In 1940 the battleship joined the rest of the Pacific Fleet in operating out of Pearl Harbor in an effort to check Japanese expansion in Asia.

The exact sequence of events leading to the *Arizona*'s loss in the first minutes of the Pearl Harbor attack has never been definitely established. The enormous explosion which destroyed the ship resulted from the ignition of the ship's forward ammunition magazine, probably as the result of a hit by an armor piercing bomb.

The force of that explosion damaged nearby ships and killed 1,177 of the *Arizona*'s complement. Her commanding officer, Captain Franklin Van Valkenburgh, and Rear Admiral Isaac Kidd, commander of Battleship Division One, were among those who perished. Both officers were awarded the Medal of Honor posthumously. The few remaining survivors aboard the ship made valiant attempts to fight the ensuing fires, but the effort was hopeless. Seeing that bravery was to no avail in the face of a blaze which would continue to burn for two days, the senior surviving officer, Lieutenant Commander Samuel Fuqua, ordered the ship abandoned. For his courage in directing firefighting and rescue activities aboard the *Arizona*, Fuqua received the Medal of Honor.

Surveys of the wreckage by divers made it apparent that the once mighty *Arizona* was too badly damaged to be raised and repaired. She was stricken from the Navy list on December 1, 1942. Work continued throughout the war to salvage whatever could be of use from the hulk. Among the items recovered were the ship's ammunition, secondary armament, electric motors and large quantities of scrap metal.

The most important items salvaged from the wreckage were the *Arizona*'s two aft turrets with their six 14-inch guns. They were transferred to the Army for use as coastal defense weapons. The Army placed one turret, named Battery Pennsylvania (the *Pennsylvania* was the *Arizona*'s sister ship), on the Mokapu Peninsula. The other turret was to be installed at Kahe Point as Battery Arizona, but the war ended before the work was complete. At Battery Pennsylvania the *Arizona*'s guns were fired only once—on the eve of Japan's surrender in 1945.

The Fleet pictured, "on guard at Pearl Harbor," in an old postcard.

Announced by invitations bearing the Secretary of the Navy's flag and the Arizona State seal, the United States Battleship Arizona's commissioning was a full–dress ceremony and a major social occasion. (bottom left)

Miss Esther Ross, of Prescott Arizona, christened the ship with a bottle of American champagne and a bottle of Arizona River water.

Thousands watched as the Arizona was launched from the Brooklyn Navy Yard on June 19, 1915. (top left)

Tugs escort the Arizona from New York Harbor for sea trials. (above) Most of the ship's superstructure was added the year following the launching.

Ford Island in 1925. The mooring quays of Battleship Row were later installed in the sheltered waters. (right foreground)

Pearl Harbor's enormous drydock could accommodate battleships like the Arizona with room to spare. Major overhauls might last two years or longer.

President Herbert Hoover, left, and Secretary of War Patrick Hurley stroll on the Arizona's deck during a Caribbean cruise in 1931. The ship had just undergone a major overhaul at the Norfolk Navy Yard.

Shipboard life was a never ending round of cleaning and maintenance. Note the enormous anchor chains.

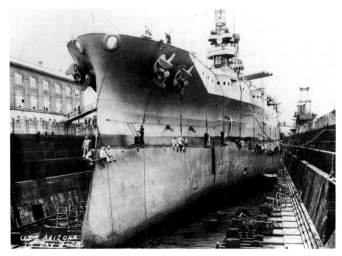

Drydocking was necessary to clean the Arizona's hull below the waterline. The ship's three anchors are visible.

Inspections were a regular feature on board ship. Failure could mean extra duty or a missed liberty.

A life vest might ensure survival in the water, but few of the Arizona's sailors had a chance to don vests when the Japanese struck on December 7, 1941.

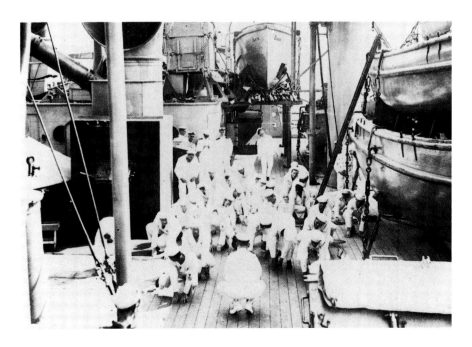

An Officer holds the attention of sailors on the Arizona's boat deck. The ship's company was formed into divisions because smaller units encouraged cohesion among the crews of large ships.

Hula dancers greet a visiting ship. (above and left) Before the Pacific Fleet was moved to Pearl Harbor in 1940, a visit to Hawaii was a major event for many Hawaii residents and U.S. sailors.

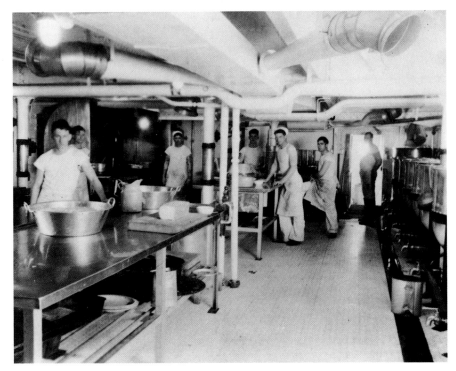

Galley crews toiled around the clock to prepare thousands of meals every day. Cleanliness was a major concern of inspecting officers who checked the food preparation compartments. Tile floor was easier to keep clean.

Souvenir shops did a brisk business with servicemen. Here a Ship's Cook First Class tries a grass skirt on for size.

Sailors on liberty shopping for ukuleles. A month's pay was often spent in a matter of hours.

The evening before the attack, the Arizona's band competed with other Pacific Fleet bands.

Two friends have their picture snapped at the beach by a sidewalk photographer.

The traditional Hawaiian welcome complete with photographer.

For a small fee, you could pose with a model in a cellophane grass skirt at a photo stand with an artificial backdrop.

A spectacular searchlight display by the Arizona and 127 other Pacific Fleet ships, 1935.

Japanese film makers built this elaborate model of Pearl Harbor for a wartime propaganda film. Battleship Row is on the right, the shipyard area at top.

The Arizona photographed in Pearl Harbor just five months before the attack.

Lord Louis Mountbatten, center, King George VI's cousin and the commander of a British aircraft carrier, visited Pearl Harbor in October 1941. He recommended that U.S. commanders in Hawaii, Lt. Gen. Walter Short, left, and Adm. Husband Kimmel, right, establish a joint Army–Navy head-quarters, but his advice was not taken. Poor inter–service coordination has since been identified as a major reason for American unpreparedness.

Oblivious to approaching disaster, downtown Honolulu decked out in Christmas lights the night before the December 7, 1941 attack.

This photo of the Fleet at anchor off Waikiki was taken by Tai Sing Loo, a photographer who witnessed the Pearl Harbor attack a short time later.

Part II: 1941–1954

Remembering Pearl Harbor

Pearl Harbor was burned into American consciousness by the shock of the nation's initial defeat and sudden entry into World War II. Few Americans who heard the news that December Sunday doubted that the nation had reached an historic turning point. That awareness, shock and thirst for revenge were expressed in the ubiquitous wartime propaganda theme "Remember Pearl Harbor." Not surprisingly, then, suggestions for a memorial to fix the event permanently in national memory appeared even before the war was over.

It is uncertain who made the first suggestion for a Pacific War Memorial. But it is known that in the fall of 1943 a civilian worker at Pearl Harbor, Tony Todaro, proposed a "Shrine of Pearl Harbor." The shrine would be a series of structures built step-like on the slopes of either Diamond Head or Punchbowl, both extinct volcanic craters in Honolulu. It would house archives relating to the Pearl Harbor attack and other Pacific War battles, as well as serve as headquarters for veterans' groups. It was to have the names of all the Pacific War dead (presumably limited to American) inscribed on its walls.

In 1944 another Pearl Harbor worker, Herbert Knowles, proposed that a memorial be built in Washington, D.C., to honor those who died on December 7, 1941. Knowles' design pursued the theme to the point of monomania. Seven steps, the number representing the day of the month of the attack, would lead to a 200-foot shaft. The base of the shaft would be forty-one feet in diameter and surrounded by twelve pillars. The shaft's width and the number of pillars alluded, of course, to the year and month of the attack. The structure would be surmounted by a clock stopped at 7:55. The proposal also called for red, white, and blue fountains and a statue of Joseph Lockhart, the radar operator whose report of the approaching Japanese raiders was ignored. Knowles planned to have the names of all of America's World War II dead inscribed on plaques in the memorial.

Todaro and Knowles put forth their ideas as individuals, but there was at least one concerted group effort toward the same end. The Pearl Harbor Memorial Trust was a coalition of Hawaii veterans and patriotic groups. They organized to raise money to build a memorial honoring all who fought in the Pacific War. The organization planned to raise funds nationwide, but the memorial would be built in Hawaii.

The authors of all three wartime plans paid tribute to the power of the memory of Pearl Harbor by including the name in all of their proposals.

Left: A mass burial for many of those killed during the attack was conducted with little ceremony at Kaneohe Naval Air Station on December 8.

Below: Smashed beyond repair, the Arizona's wreckage lies in the mud at the bottom of Pearl Harbor.

Three photos taken from Japanese planes during the attack. Ford Island and Battleship Row (above and far right) before the heaviest damage.

Leaking oil from ships' fuel tanks was soon spreading over the harbor. Within minutes the fuel was ablaze, hampering rescue operations and threatening undamaged ships.

Wheeler Field, (right) where U.S. fighter planes were destroyed before they could get off the ground.

The explosion of the USS Shaw's forward magazines, one of the war's most famous photographs. Debris from the blast landed half a mile away.

Concentric waves in the water by Battleship Row indicate a near miss. Fuel oil is visible on the surface of the water. It will soon be ablaze.

At the height of the attack, a flight of B–17's en route from California to the Philippines arrived. Stripped of their machine guns to save weight and fuel during the long flight, the bombers were no match for Japanese Zeroes. Miraculously, most made safe landings at Hickam Field (shown here) and other airfields around Ohau. One made an emergency landing on a golf course.

The West Virginia, left, was sunk by torpedos, but the Tennessee was protected by her inboard mooring position.

Caught by surprise, Navy patrol planes such as these PBY's were destroyed on the ground. Sailors and other servicemen performed heroically fighting fires and pulling undamaged aircraft to safety.

Desperate attempts to cope amid smoke and fire at Ford Island Naval Air Station. Emergency sprinklers in the main fuel tanks prevented a worse disaster.

"On the 6th of December, Saturday afternoon, I had made arrangement with Tech Sergeant Christen to have all his Guard be at the main gate between 8:30 to 9:30 o'clock Sunday morning to have a group of pictures taken in front of the new concrete entrance as a setting with the 'Pearl Harbor' for Christmas card to send home to their family.

"Sunday morning I left home for Pearl Harbor after 7:00 o'clock ... When I approach Pearl Harbor surprise with great shock. Thought one of oil tanks caught in fire, showing black volume of thick smoke in the air ... I was great shock with surprise the war are on. Watching many Japanese war planes attack Pearl Harbor, dropping bombs right and left on dry docks and Ford Island. Suddenly terrific explosion.-Fire broke out ... I wish my Graflex with me ...

"The Marines of the fire dept. of the Navy Yard are the Heros of the Day of Dec. 7, 1941..."

Tai Sing Loo, *a shipyard photographer who witnessed the attack.*

The Arizona's forward magazine exploding in a ball of fire. The moment was captured on film by a Navy doctor from the deck of the hospital ship Solace.

Sailors abandoning ship after the USS California was struck by torpedoes. Manholes in the fuel and void compartments had been opened in anticipation of an inspection, and this increased flooding below decks.

Although the Arizona was destroyed almost instantly, fires from the initial explosion burned for three days.

Ships in Hawaiian Waters
December 7, 1941

Allen (DD–66)	PT–30
Antares (AKS–3)	PT–42
Argonne (AG–31)	Patterson (DD–392)
Arizona (BB–39)	Pelias (AS–14)
Ash (YN–2)	Pennsylvania (BB–38)
Avocet (AVP–4)	Perry (DMS–17)
Aylwin (DD–355)	Phelps (DD–360)
Bagley (DD–386)	Phoenix (CL–46)
Blue (DD–387)	Preble (DM–20)
Bobolink (AM–20)	Pruitt (DM–22)
Breese (DM–18)	Pyro (AE–1)
CG–8 (USCG)	Rail (AM–26)
Cachalot (SS–170)	Raleigh (CL–7)
California (BB–44)	Ralph Talbot (DD–390)
Case (DD–370)	Ramapo (AO–12)
Cassin (DD–372)	Ramsay (DM–16)
Castor (AKS–1)	Reedbird (AMc–30)
Chengho (IX–52)	Reid (DD–369)
Chew (DD–106)	Reliance (USCG)
Cinchona (YN–7)	Rigel (AR–11)
Cockatoo (AMc–8)	St. Louis (CL–49)
Cockenoe (YN–47)	Sacramento (PG–19)
Condor (AMc–14)	San Francisco (CA–38)
Conyngham (DD–371)	Schley (DD–103)
Crossbill (AMc–9)	Selfridge (DD–357)
Cummings (DD–365)	Shaw (DD–373)
Curtiss (AV–4)	Sicard (DM–21)
Dale (DD–353)	Solace (AH–5)
Detroit (CL–8)	Sotoyomo (YT–9)
Dewey (DD–349)	Sumner (AG–32)
Dobbin (AD–3)	Sunnadin (AT–28)
Dolphin (SS–169)	Swan (AVP–7)
Downes (DD–375)	Taney (PG–37)(USCG)
Farragut (DD–348)	Tangier (AV–8)
Gamble (DM–15)	Tautog (SS–199)
Grebe (AM–43)	Tennessee (BB–43)
Helena (CL–50)	Tern (AM–31)
Helm (DD–388)	Thornton (AVD–11)
Henley (DD–391)	Tiger (PC–152)(USCG)
Hoga (YT–146)	Trever (DMS–16)
Honolulu (CL–48)	Tracy (DM–19)
Hulbert (AVD–6)	Tucker (DD–374)
Hull (DD–350)	Turkey (AM–13)
Jarvis (DD–393)	Utah (AG–16)
Keosangua (AT–38)	Vega (AK–17)
MacDonough (DD–351)	Vestal (AR–4)
Manuwai (YFB–17)	Vireo (AM–52)
Marin (YN–53)	Wapello (YN–56)
Maryland (BB–46)	Ward (DD–139)
Medusa (AR–1)	Wasmuth (DMS–15)
Monaghan (DD–354)	West Virginia (BB–48)
Montgomery (DM–17)	Whitney (AD–4)
Mugford (DD–389)	Widgeon (ASR–1)
Narwhal (SS–167)	Worden (DD–352)
Navajo (AT–64)	YG–15
Neosho (AO–23)	YG–17
Nevada (BB–36)	YG–21
New Orleans (CA–32)	YMT–5
Nokomis (YT–142)	YNg–17
Oglala (CM–4)	YO–21
Oklahoma (BB–37)	YO–30
Ontaria (AT–13)	YO–43
Osceola (YT–129)	YO–44
PT–20	YP–108
PT–21	YP–109
PT–22	YTT–3
PT–23	YT–119
PT–24	YT–130
PT–25	YT–152
PT–26	YT–153
PT–27	YW–16
PT–28	Zane (DMS–14)
PT–29	

Small craft of every description helped rescue survivors, transport wounded, aid the ships, and fight fires. Many were strafed by Japanese planes.

The old minelayer, Oglala, capsized and sank after a torpedo hit the neighboring cruiser, Helena. A civilian tugboat pulled the Oglala clear of the Helena before the Oglala turned over completely.

The sight of the overturned Oklahoma demoralized many sailors who had refused to believe a battleship could capsize.

Righting the overturned Oklahoma was a major engineering feat. Winches installed on Ford Island (above) were connected to pully structures welded to the ship's hull. (below) The Oklahoma, which proved to be beyond repair, was sold for scrap and sank at sea on the way to the scrapyard.

After the attack, only the Arizona's superstructure remained above water. Salvage vessels began work on the wreckage almost immediately. By the end of 1942, virtually everything above the main deck had been removed for scrap or use on other ships.

Cameraman Al Brick documenting the destruction at Wheeler Field on movie film. On the runway is a wrecked amphibian plane.

Children examining the wreckage of a downed Japanese plane. Only 29 Japanese aircraft were shot down by U.S. fighters and antiaircraft fire—less than ten percent of the attacking force.

KILLED AND WOUNDED IN THE ATTACK:

NAVY 2,008 killed, 710 wounded
ARMY 218 killed, 364 wounded
MARINES 109 killed, 69 wounded
CIVILIANS 68 killed, 35 wounded
TOTALS 2,403 killed, 1,178 wounded
(Exact figures for Japanese killed and wounded unknown)

Sixty–eight civilian deaths occurred as a result of the attack. In civilian areas like this, heavy damage was attributed to falling U.S. antiaircraft fire.

The Royal Hawaiian Hotel and Waikiki
Beach strung with barbed wire in anticipation of a Japanese invasion. Sunbathers
used the wire to hang wet bathing things to
dry. The Japanese never invaded.

Destroyers Cassin and Downes were caught in Drydock Number 1. Behind them is the
damaged Battleship Pennsylvania.

Mess Attendant Doris Miller wearing the Navy Cross he won for heroism aboard the USS West Virginia during the Pearl Harbor attack. Navy policy at the time restricted blacks to menial jobs, but Miller manned an antiaircraft machine gun on the ship while it was being bombed and strafed by Japanese planes. Although he survived Pearl Harbor, he was killed in action in 1943 during the invasion of the Gilbert Islands.

In anticipation of a Japanese invasion, U.S. troops install barbed wire around Iolani Palace, the seat of Hawaii's territorial government.

Salvage work on the Arizona was difficult and dangerous. For protection against poisonous gases, workers wore face masks and respirators as they removed ammunition.

Servicemen and women gathered at the base of Aloha Tower, a Honolulu landmark camouflaged during the war years. Hawaii was a staging ground for hundreds of thousands of military personnel on their way to forward areas in the Pacific Theater.

Workers labored into the night of December 7th to repair damage at Hickam Field.

After Pearl Harbor, the Army turned the lei–making skills of these Hawaiian women to the production of camouflage nets.

Sandbags, furniture, and a wrecked airplane engine form a makeshift observation post at Hickam Field. The Japanese did not attack again, but Hawaii was not militarily secure until the U.S. victory at the Midway six months after Pearl Harbor.

Delirious crowds jammed downtown Honolulu when news of Japan's defeat began to spread.

Jubilant servicemen hoist bottles and the headlines as they ride through the streets of Honolulu. Most of these men would soon be returning home to make the postwar readjustment to civilian life.

The Pacific War Memorial Commission

The war over, public interest in a Pacific War Memorial faded as attention in Hawaii and the mainland U.S. shifted to postwar concerns. But a few years later interest began to revive. In 1949 the Territory of Hawaii established the Pacific War Memorial Commission, an agency authorized to plan and raise funds for the erection of war memorials in the territory.

The commission was composed of seven unpaid members who collectively represented the business community, Hawaii's social elite, and the Islands' Japanese-American veterans. It was chaired by H. Tucker Gratz, a man with solid political connections and formidable diplomatic skills. He was at various times in his career a naval officer, a businessman, and a federal official. The talents of Gratz and the other commissioners would be taxed, for the commission received virtually no operating funds from the territorial government.

The commission's enabling legislation charged it with duties relating to war memorials. However, the Territorial government originally envisioned a very different collateral, perhaps even primary duty for the PWMC. It was directed to serve as liaison with the Pacific War Memorial, Inc., a private nonprofit group formed to sponsor a wide variety of scientific research activities in the Pacific Basin.

The Pacific War Memorial, Inc., seemed to promise great things for Hawaii. Its board of directors included a thick slice of the Eastern establishment: Henry Stimson, William Donovan, Oveta Culp Hobby, Artemus Gates, and a sprinkling of Roosevelts and Rockefellers. There was talk of locating the organization's field headquarters in Honolulu, with no telling how much money and prestige might accrue to Hawaii.

As fate would have it, though, the promise of the Pacific War Memorial, Inc., never materialized. The PWMC turned its attention to consideration of war memorial structures for Hawaii. In 1951 the commissioners arrived at a conception for an entire system of memorials. It would include sites and structures at Red Hill, the Marine parade ground, the main gate of Pearl Harbor Naval Station, the wreckage of the USS *Arizona,* and a connecting boulevard between Nimitz and Kamehameha Highways.

The commission's plan called for a permanent platform over the ship. It would be connected by a ramp to Ford Island, where there would be an observation tower, archives, and a museum. A Territorial legislator speaking on the commission's behalf affirmed, "the *Arizona* is very much a factor in any memorial system that is desired."

The PWMC did not, of course, operate in a vacuum. It is impossible to say who first thought of the idea of a memorial at the *Arizona,* but as early as 1946 Tucker Gratz had been struck by the neglect of the sunken battleship when he visited the wreckage to place a wreath on the anniversary of the attack, only to find the dead wreath he had put there the previous December 7. At the same time the Navy commands at Pearl Harbor were well aware of the *Arizona*'s presence and bothered by the lack of tangible acknowledgement of its significance.

In the early 1950s, as the PWMC was formulating its proposals, others were making their own plans for the *Arizona.* On March 7, 1950, Admiral Arthur Radford, commander-in-chief of the Pacific Fleet, caused a flagstaff to be installed on the protruding base of the hulk's rear mast. At the same time he ordered that the American flag be raised and lowered daily. Later that year a wooden platform was built over the amidships area. On the ninth anniversary of the attack a commemorative metal plaque was installed at the base of the flagstaff and another welded to the deck of the wreck of the target ship USS *Utah.* Radford envisioned these steps as stopgap preliminaries to a permanent solution to the problem of ignominious deterioration and ordered a study on "rehabilitating" the *Arizona.*

Right: *Admiral Arthur Radford at the ceremony dedicating the flagstaff he had placed on the Arizona's severed mainmast. Although the ship is no longer in commission, a color guard raises and lowers the flag daily.*

Ceremonies being conducted at the first Arizona Memorial—a temporary platform.

Another view of the first Memorial installed by the Navy in 1950 over the Arizona's wreckage. Circular structures are foundations for the aft gun turrets.

National Interest

On the mainland, too, there was interest in the *Arizona*. *Collier's* magazine printed an editorial calling for a memorial over the ship as "a fitting tribute to the men of the *Arizona*, and to the others who died at Pearl Harbor and Hickam Field."

Congressman Thomas Lane of Massachusetts submitted bills in 1950 and 1951 to authorize a "shrine" at the *Arizona* so "we shall be awakened to the need of protecting [freedom] from the lurking enemies who would corrupt, undermine, and destroy man's last best hope on earth." The Navy Club of the United States suggested a bronze marker on the *Arizona's* hull "commemorating Pearl Harbor Day."

With such widespread interest the PWMC began to think of the fundraising required to build its memorial system. Greatly overoptimistic, the commissioners seriously underestimated the difficulty of raising money from private donors. There

Artist's rendering of an early plan for the Memorial. The Navy rejected this idea because visitor facilities were located on Ford Island.

were sanguine estimates that $10,000,000 might be raised by such means as the sale of vanda orchids on the mainland.

Then reality closed in. The early flurry of interest failed to generate enough momentum to make a serious start. For one thing, there was no meeting of the minds on *why* there should be a memorial. Radford and other officers at Pearl Harbor saw an *Arizona* memorial as a Navy obligation to what had been one of the fleet's proudest ships and the sailors who went down with her. *Collier's* editors viewed the issue as basically one of marking the graves of all American servicemen killed in the attack. Congressman Lane, riding the flood tide of McCarthyism, wanted an opportunity to remind Americans of the dangers of internal subversion. The Navy Club wanted to recognize December 7, 1941, as a decisive date in American history. With such a diversity of motives it is little wonder that the project was foundering in the early 1950s.

There were also other, less abstract, reasons for the failure to raise signifcant amount of funds. Congressional budget restrictions during that period virtually guaranteed that "frills" such as an *Arizona* memorial stood no chance of federal funding. In addition, security regulations then in force barred the general public from Pearl Harbor. Who would expect a Congressional appropriation for a monument which most taxpayers could not visit?

Finally, a decade after the most spectacular defeat in U.S. military history there remained a deep reluctance on the part of many to recall that occasion. *Collier's* felt that the Navy's hesitation to press for an appropriation stemmed less from tight budgets than to a desire to forget a shameful defeat.

In response to a request that he proclaim December 7 a "national day of prayer" President Harry S. Truman replied that the anniversary of the attack should be remembered, if at all, "only as a day of infamy." At least one member of the PWMC shared those sentiments and objected to the commission's planned observances on December 7 as "uncalled for."

The time for constructing an *Arizona* memorial was not quite ripe, but the idea was not dead. It would not be long before proponents would once again marshal their resources and conduct a successful effort to realize their goal.

A Dive Into History

Special Supplement

Underwater Archeology of the USS Arizona

The fires on the USS *Arizona* had barely cooled when navy divers began salvage operations on the battleship. Within a week of the Pearl Harbor attack divers had entered the after part of the ship and made a preliminary survey of her condition and the location of valuables. In subsequent months they removed unexploded ammunition from the after magazines and stripped away most of the superstructure for use as scrap.

There was a special urgency to these wartime efforts. Hawaii's defenders, expecting the December 7th attack to be followed by a Japanese invasion, were desperate for any kind of defensive armament. To meet the urgent need the *Arizona*'s two after 14-inch gun turrets were removed and turned over to the army for use as coastal defense weapons.

Salvage officers ultimately concluded that the battleship could not be raised and returned to service, so it was decommissioned on December 1, 1942. After all usable material had been recovered from the hulk, salvage operations were abandoned in late 1943. The wreckage remained largely undisturbed until 1962, when the USS *Arizona* Memorial was constructed. The passing years have seen ever increasing numbers of visitors drawn to this reminder of America's entry into the Second World War.

After assuming responsibility for visitor operations at the *Arizona* Memorial in 1980, the National Park Service faced a growing number of questions about the condition of the *Arizona* wreckage. What portions of the ship actually remained? Was the structure deteriorating? And most importantly, was there any danger that the hull would shift its position and endanger the memorial?

Opposite: Perspective view drawing from bow of the submerged USS Arizona.

Below: One of the Arizona's 14-inch guns dwarfs a National Park service diver. These cannon could fire a 1,000 pound projectile over 10 miles. The forward guns (including this one) are still intact; those in the ship's other three turrets were removed in 1942.

Left: *A bowl and fork lying on the deck of what was once the Arizona's galley.*

Right: *The remains of a stove in the crew's galley. The Arizona's cooks and bakers worked to feed an endless line of hungry men who streamed into the galley at all hours of the day and night.*

To answer those questions the Park Service undertook an underwater archeological survey in 1983 and 1984. Divers accomplished the work in two phases lasting two weeks each. The operation, carried out by U.S. Navy and Park Service divers, was funded by a $39,000 grant from the *Arizona* Memorial Museum Association.

The National Park Service set several objectives for the survey:

- To fix the *Arizona*'s position, make an accurate chart of the wreckage, and identify damaged areas.
- To establish permanent reference point markers on the hull to identify any future shifting or settling.
- To place permanent reference point markers on the hull to identify any future shifting or settling.
- To determine the extent and effects of saltwater corrosion and the growth of coral and other marine organisms on the *Arizona*'s hull.
- To locate the opening through which oil still seeps to the surface from the ship's fuel tanks.
- To search for torpedo damage to the battleship. World War II navy divers were unable to find any evidence of an underwater hit, but eyewitnesses to the Pearl Harbor attack claim she was struck by at least one Japanese torpedo.

It was decided at the outset of the project that divers would confine their activities to the outside of the battleship and would not enter the hull. The decision was based on two factors: respect for the dead entombed in the ship, and the danger of divers becoming trapped or injured in the interior wreckage.

Diving operations began on September 20, 1983, with a sweep of the deck and nearby harbor bottom by divers from the navy's explosive ordnance disposal (EOD) unit at Pearl Harbor. The EOD divers proved the wisdom of the precaution when they discovered and safely disposed of four live 5-inch antiaircraft rounds on the *Arizona*'s deck.

The project stimulated intense news media coverage, and diving operations were conducted in full view of thousands of daily visitors to the *Arizona* Memorial. As the divers progressed with the survey they meticulously documented their findings with photographs, videotapes, and drawings. The drawings proved to be especially important, because poor underwater visibility (due to suspended silt particles) made it impossible to take clear photographs.

Beginning their survey of the wreckage from the battleship's bow, the divers found the first 20 feet of the ship relatively undamaged. But the next 200 feet (roughly one-third of her length) was devastated by the forward ammunition magazine explosion which sank the *Arizona*. Divers found it unrecognizable as a warship; it appeared "merely [as] irregular mounds of metal and coral rising twenty feet from the mud bottom."[1] So great was the force of explosion that it collapsed the deck nearly 30 feet, distended the ship's forecastle width by several feet, and opened a 2-inch crack which ran completely down one side and partially up the other side of the thickly armored hull.

Surmounting this destruction, the underwater explorers discovered the battleship's Number One (foremost) 14-inch gun turret eerily intact. The three giant guns were trained forward in near perfect alignment as if they were manned and awaiting only the order to fire. More than 40 years after the *Arizona*'s death, however, the turret lay nearly 30 feet below its original position, her only foe the relentless and irresistable force of saltwater corrosion.

Left: *This frame once supported a canvas awning which shaded the rectangular hatchway below. As Japanese bombers pounded the Arizona, crewmen rushed through this and other hatches to man their battle stations. When it was clear the vessel was lost sailors streamed from their posts below decks to abandon ship.*

Right: *As the Arizona sank, her crew tried valiantly to fight the fires which engulfed the ship. This coupling connected two lengths of firehose which still lie on the ship's deck.*

1. John Martini, "Surveying the Arizona," *After The Battle*, No. 45 (Aug. 1984), 41

As the divers worked their way aft they discovered other features which recalled the chaos and fury of the December 7th attack: a porthole with its unbroken glass cover still in place; broken crockery in the ship's galley; firehoses strewn about the deck in a futile effort to contain the fires ignited by Japanese bombs; and open hatches through which the *Arizona*'s crew rushed to their battle stations that long ago morning. Most dramatic of all were the holes where armor piercing bombs penetrated the *Arizona*'s hull.

These scenes were fascinating and moving, but the dives were no mere sight-seeing tour. They were a scientific archeological survey, and the divers made important findings which have aided the National Park Service in managing the USS *Arizona* Memorial and interpreting the site to visitors. The accomplishments of the underwater survey include:

- The mapping of the vessel and the compilation of drawings and photographs into accurate renderings of the USS *Arizona*'s remains.
- The establishment of reference points and base lines to measure future changes in the hull's position and condition.
- The discovery that the process of saltwater corrosion apparently poses no immediate danger to the ship or its stability, and that the growth of coral on some sections actually serves to retard the corrosion.
- Divers were unable to determine whether the *Arizona* was struck by a torpedo. This ship has settled in more than 20 feet of mud, which makes examination of her bottom impossible.
- The source of leaking oil was found to be near the Number Three gun turret. The rate of seepage was measured at four drops per minute.

The National Park Service plans future dives on the ship to learn more about the hull and to measure changes in its condition. Until then the *Arizona* will rest in peace.

Left above: *The sunken Arizona serves as a home to fish, coral, and other forms of marine life which inhabit the waters of Pearl Harbor. The vessel provides a reef-like environment which attracts many of the same species found on Hawaii's natural reefs.*

Left below: *Survey divers carefully measure base lines which will be used to study changes in the Arizona's condition. The growth encrusted on the ship's surface protects the hull from salt water corrosion.*

Above: *The Arizona today gives only a glimpse of what lies below the surface.*

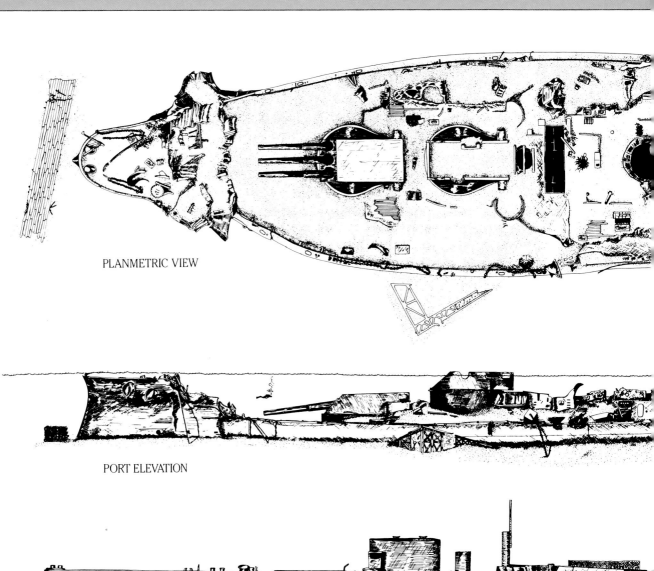

PLANMETRIC VIEW

PORT ELEVATION

STARBOARD ELEVATION

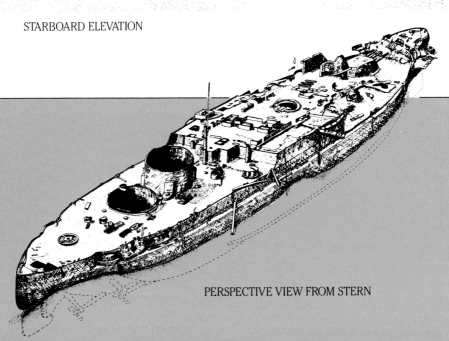

PERSPECTIVE VIEW FROM STERN

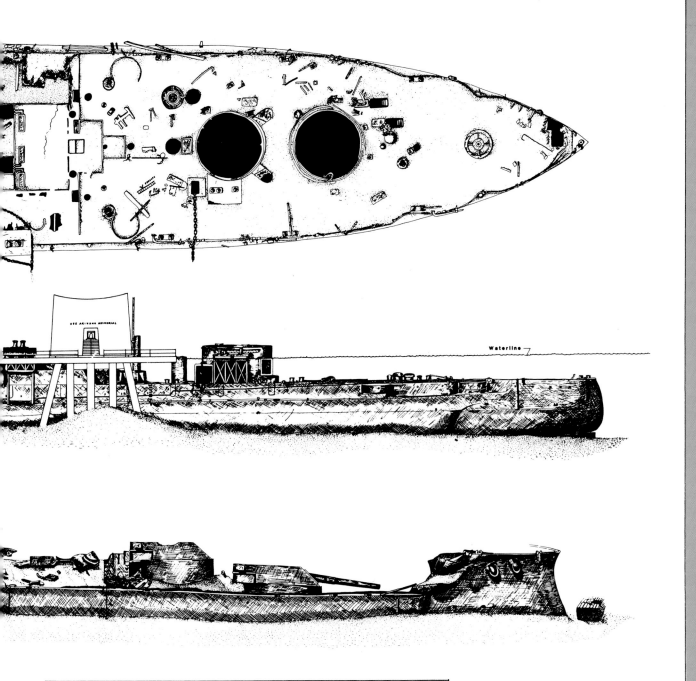

USS Arizona

U.S. National Park Service
Submerged Cultural Resources Unit

Detailed drawings of the USS Arizona were one result of the underwater archeological survey of the ship. The port elevation rendering (center) shows the battleship in relation to the waterline, and the location of the Arizona Memorial structure.

Part III: 1955–1962

Navy Overtures

The first sign that an *Arizona* memorial might become a reality came in 1955. On December 7 of that year the Navy Club dedicated on Ford Island, near the *Arizona,* a ten-foot-high basalt stone with a plaque dedicated to the memory of American servicemen killed in the December 7, 1941, attack. It was the first permanent memorial at Pearl Harbor.

While the Navy Club marker was being installed, the command at Pearl Harbor renewed its own efforts. Two weeks before the dedication of the Navy Club monument, the Commandant of the Fourteenth Naval District (the command responsible for Pearl Harbor and other Navy bases in Hawaii) wrote the Secretary of the Navy regarding the matter. He pointed out the need for a memorial over the remains of the *Arizona:*

> Whether or not the Navy has done its best to preserve the dignity of the *Arizona*'s remains, it is still blamed because this burial place for 1,102 men is a rusted mass of junk . . .
> . . . an appropriate memorial should be constructed to honor the many valiant men who went down with her and who now lie entombed within her hull.

The sentiment was endorsed by the Chief of Naval Operations, Admiral Arleigh Burke, and Fleet Admiral Chester Nimitz, World War II commander of the Pacific Fleet and honorary chairman of the PWMC. Despite those weighty endorsements, there was no immediate action forthcoming at the Cabinet or Congressional level.

The Navy was resolved, and began to explore alternative routes to its goal. In early 1956 Commander Jay Smith, a Fourteenth Naval District staff officer, approached the PWMC for help. He noted that the Navy Club was looking into the possibility of raising funds nationally for an *Arizona* memorial. Would the PWMC participate, too? The commission mulled over the request. In May, when Navy Secretary Charles Thomas publicly endorsed the Navy Club campaign, the PWMC offered to work with that organization. Responding to that offer, the Fourteenth District Commandant made a formal request to the PWMC to raise funds for an *Arizona* memorial.

It soon became apparent that, for reasons not clear, the Navy Club would be unable to fulfill its commitment. The commission then faced the question of whether to undertake the campaign on its own. It was not an easy decision. At that time Hawaii was considerably more isolated—both psychologically and in terms of travel time—from the mainland United States than it would be after the advent of statehood (1959), jet passenger service, and mass tourism. But the big question was, could a group working from Hawaii command the national attention and credibility needed for such a task?

Left: Crew of the USS Bennington assembled on deck to spell out a tribute to the Arizona as they pass the sunken ship, Memorial Day, 1958.

Below: Dignitaries gather to pay homage to the USS Arizona's dead.

After studying the problems of fundraising, its legal mandate and the advantages of Navy backing, the commission decided to proceed with the project. One of its first actions was to establish an *Arizona* Memorial fund trust account at the Bishop Trust Company. It then secured the agreement of the Post Office to route mail addressed to "USS *Arizona*, Pearl Harbor, Hawaii" to Bishop Trust.

Authorizing Legislation

After deciding to proceed with the project, the PWMC and the Navy encountered problems no one had considered. First, the Navy had no legal authority to accept money from the PWMC for the memorial. Second, even if it could accept the money, the Navy had no authority to erect a memorial over the *Arizona.*

It would require an act of Congress to win an exemption from the principle that federal agencies could be funded only from the federal treasury. An even stickier point was the jealously guarded prerogative of the American Battle Monuments Commission (ABMC). The ABMC was a federal agency charged with erecting war memorials such as the one proposed for the *Arizona.* It was no lightweight organization; it included General of the Army George C. Marshall, as well as members of both houses of Congress.

The drive for legislative exemptions was made difficult by the fact that the PWMC had to rely mainly on John Burns, Hawaii's single Delegate to Congress, who did not have a vote. However, Burns turned to the task with a will and a large fund of political common sense. In January 1957 he introduced HR 5809, which would provide the necessary authority for the Navy to build the memorial, to accept funds from the PWMC, and to give the commission incidental assistance during the fundraising drive. He was careful to draft the bill so that it could not possibly be construed to authorize the expenditure of federal funds for the memorial. He continually emphasized that selling point in public and private discussion.

In addition, he obtained from the Navy a list of *Arizona* casualties and their home towns. His staff proceeded to break down the list by Congressional districts, and Burns provided every Congressman with a list of crew members from his or her district who had been killed on the battleship on December 7, 1941. That this touch provided a powerful incentive to support the bill was attested to by, among others, Representative Barratt O'Hara of Illinois, who told his colleagues:

> … in reminding us that among the heroes of the nation … were some who had been our constituents, the gentleman from Hawaii gave us the added personal sense that in supporting HR 5809 we were aiding in building a memorial not only for our countrymen personally unknown to us but also for the members of our own community families.

Burns knew that, as in the early 1950s, many people who were inclined to support a bill to authorize the *Arizona* Memorial would have widely varying and emotionally charged opinions on the need for a memorial.

The Commandant of the Fourteenth Naval district, as noted above, seemed at least as concerned with the disgraceful spectacle of the *Arizona's* deteriorating remains as with the memory of those killed in the attack.

The Commandant of the Marine Corps, General R. McC. Pate wrote, "Besides memorializing the brave men who lost their lives at Pearl Harbor, such a shrine will serve as a reminder of the courage, hardship and sacrifice [required] to bring World War II to a successful conclusion."

The senior surviving officer aboard the *Arizona* during the attack, Rear Admiral Samuel Fuqua, saw the issue as being one of providing "a suitable resting place" for his late shipmates.

Fuqua's feelings struck a responsive chord in H. Tucker Gratz and the Navy's Chief of Legislative Liaison, Rear Admiral E. C. Stephan. They saw the memorial as "a fitting tribute to the personnel of the USS *Arizona* who gave their lives…and whose remains have not been and cannot be recovered from the hull."

Memorial services for Pearl Harbor dead. White crosses and stars of David mark many grave sites.

Decorating graves at Oahu Cemetery after the attack on Pearl Harbor. During the war years, children wore gas masks strapped over their shoulders.

Admiral Burke thought of it as commemorating "all American servicemen who lost their lives in the Pacific area during World War II and it will remind the people of the Free World that they must never allow an attack such as that which sank the *Arizona* to reoccur."

Burke's afterthought found amplification in Congress. This was the period of President Dwight D. Eisenhower's "bigger bang for the buck" defense policy with its reliance on strategic nuclear weaponry. The year Burns introduced the *Arizona* Memorial bill saw the climax of the race between the United States and the Soviet Union to build the first Intercontinental Ballistic Missile. The potential for a surprise attack that would dwarf the results of the Japanese raid on Pearl Harbor was frighteningly obvious. Senator Carl Hayden of Arizona vented a full charge of Cold War rhetoric in support of the bill:

> . . . it is imperative that we be prepared either to win a war against Godless communism or to prevent such a war by being so strong that the dictators in Moscow will be afraid to drop the first bomb. It is, therefore, appropriate that, through this memorial, we focus our attention on our most striking example of unpreparedness, so that we may be perpetually reminded of the security that is found in strength.

There were those who felt it would not do to push that theme too far. Admiral Nimitz, whose cooperation in the fundraising drive was vital, had a strong distaste for dwelling on the day that the fleet was crushed by surprise attack. "I have always regretted," he wrote, "that we memorialize Pearl Harbor Day—which was a great defeat for us."

It was important to keep supporters, both in and out of Congress, from becoming embroiled needlessly in conflicting interpretations of the need for a memorial. Burns solved that problem neatly when he drafted the bill. He avoided any preamble or clauses justifying the need for a memorial. The measure contained no unnecessary verbiage or references to who or what would be memorialized, just a cleanly written text to authorize "a United States Ship *Arizona* Memorial at Pearl Harbor."

It was well that Burns had done his political spadework, exercised careful draftsmanship, and avoided clashes about appropriations and metaphysics. The American Battle Monuments Commission was ready with objections to this intrusion into its domain. Senator Charles Potter of Michigan, an ABMC member, spoke against the bill, opposing it on two counts.

First he said, "This proposal relates to what is essentially a Navy ship. We are considering what really is a one-service affair." The ABMC knew from experience how easily inter- or intraservice jealousies could mar a memorial project if one ship, unit or service felt that the sacrifices of its members or crew had been slighted in inscriptions, statuary, or a host of other symbolic representations. That jealousy could linger like a pall over public attitudes toward a memorial long after the structure had been completed.

Second, Potter cautioned, too many monuments had been erected by individual units or services. Those who built them rarely thought of the need for routine maintenance and upkeep. Most had deteriorated disgracefully. The ABMC was established, he pointed out, to deal with precisely that problem. It had the experience and institutional resources to guarantee permanent upkeep. Therefore, he concluded, functions such as the building of the *Arizona* Memorial were rightly, and for good reason, the province of his commission.

Potter's qualms about the problems of upkeep were given little weight by his colleagues. Senator Leverett Saltonstall of Massachusetts responded offhandedly, "The Navy estimates that the cost of maintaining such a memorial will be no more than the cost it now incurs in maintaining the battleship *Arizona* in its present condition."

The work of Burns and his allies had been thorough. Potter was the only member of either house to speak on the floor against the bill. Seeing that he had little chance of defeating it with delaying tactics, he declined the chance to try to kill the measure by "amending it to death."

PWMC chairman Tucker Gratz, a naval reserve officer, had arranged for temporary active duty in Washington while the bill made its way through Congress. He watched from the Senate gallery as it passed on final vote. The measure was signed into law as Public Law 85-344 on March 15, 1958.

Workers driving the end pilings that will support the Memorial's bridge–like structure.

The Arizona Memorial nearing completion. Scaffolding supported forms for poured concrete.

Fundraising

W ith legal authorization secured, the PWMC was faced with the reality of actually raising funds to build the *Arizona* Memorial. Immediately the commission had to confront the disadvantages of being based in a distant island territory of the United States and the problems of long distance fundraising. The unpaid citizens who formed the commission were unable to undertake the demanding responsibility of operating a national fundraising drive on a day-to-day basis. At that point they sought a professional fundraiser.

After a period of deliberation, the commissioners selected Darrel Brady, a Southern California fundraiser and publicist. Brady had worked with Tucker Gratz for the Boy Scouts of America before the war, and the commission followed his recommendation in selecting a professional coordinator for the national campaign.

On June 16, 1958, Brady contracted with the PWMC to conduct the national campaign in return for a 15 percent commission on all monies raised for the PWMC's *Arizona* Memorial fund. The agreement was to run for 18 months and was later extended to July 31, 1960. Brady's firm, Darrel Brady Associates, was to bear all operating expenses.

The relationship between Brady and the commission was not a happy one. Some degree of tension and minor disagreements were perhaps inevitable in any relationship between a distant fundraiser-publicist and a commission growing nervous about the stories filtering back about their loosely supervised agent. Brady often proclaimed exaggerated fundraising goals and too seldom delivered on promises that major breakthroughs were just around the corner. Many times he assured the commissioners that he was on the brink of enlisting decisive support from unspecified prominent figures and organizations. That support never materialized. Even more troublesome, he did not always exercise good judgment in selecting local area coordinators for the campaign.

Brady's methods seemed odd, even amateurish. His approach is suggested by his first proposal to the PWMC. He envisioned a giant piggy bank which would be trailered from place to place to solicit donations for the *Arizona* Memorial from people throughout the country.

Brady's goals were also wildly exaggerated. The PWMC originally estimated a $250,000 cost for the memorial. But recognizing that such projects had a tendency to run over the estimated costs and to allow for some shortfall in effort, the commission set a target of $500,000. Brady, however, took the bit between his teeth and announced a goal of $2,000,000. He proclaimed it not only to the commission but caused embarrassment by spreading the exaggerated figure among national publications, veterans' groups, and public officials.

The commission remonstrated gently at first: "your proposal for a $2,000,000 goal leaves us a little breathless;...our goal is a more modest $500,000." When Brady persisted, the tone became icier: "Such a figure has no foundation in fact. Such statements can not only be misleading and confusing...they can be most damaging both to the commission and the campaign."

The commission's dissatisfaction was evident in a February 1959 letter from Joe Custer, its executive secretary, to Brady. Custer pointed out that the fund was only at the halfway mark to the commission's goal, and that most donations to date had come from members of military units, veterans' groups, and patriotic organizations. The inference was clear that those sources needed little selling and probably would have donated whether or not Brady had been involved.

The commissioners' frustration with Brady's failure to deliver is evident in file memos. Gratz wrote, "Brady has failed to answer my questions satisfactorily and therefore has nothing definite lined up." Another commissioner complained of Brady's "far too nebulous" promises.

Brady, for his part, felt that despite his 15 percent commission, his best efforts were unappreciated. He claimed to be $30,000 in debt as a result of expenses incurred in the *Arizona* Memorial campaign and appealed to the commission to overlook the contract clause which obligated him to bear all operating expenses. He asked for at least partial reimbursement. If he was not reimbursed, he threatened, his creditors would take the attitude that "'the Pacific War Memorial

Right: *Elvis Presley poster announcing his 1961 benefit performance for the Arizona Memorial fund.*

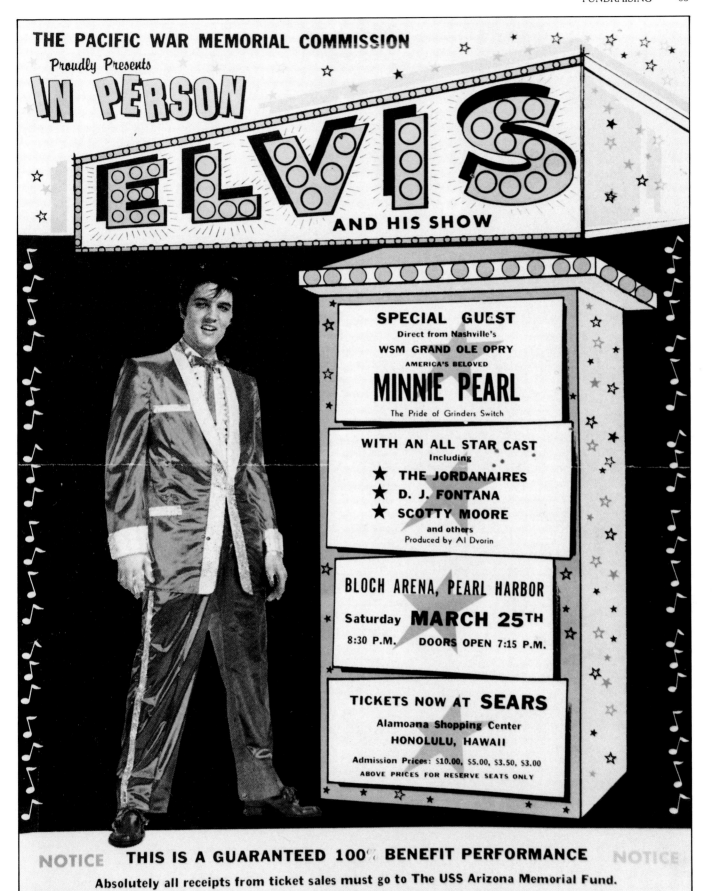

THE PACIFIC WAR MEMORIAL COMMISSION

Proudly Presents

IN PERSON

ELVIS

AND HIS SHOW

SPECIAL GUEST
Direct from Nashville's
WSM GRAND OLE OPRY
AMERICA'S BELOVED
MINNIE PEARL
The Pride of Grinders Switch

WITH AN ALL STAR CAST
Including
★ THE JORDANAIRES
★ D. J. FONTANA
★ SCOTTY MOORE
and others
Produced by Al Dvorin

BLOCH ARENA, PEARL HARBOR
Saturday MARCH 25TH
8:30 P.M.   DOORS OPEN 7:15 P.M.

TICKETS NOW AT SEARS
Alamoana Shopping Center
HONOLULU, HAWAII
Admission Prices: $10.00, $5.00, $3.50, $3.00
ABOVE PRICES FOR RESERVE SEATS ONLY

NOTICE   THIS IS A GUARANTEED 100% BENEFIT PERFORMANCE   NOTICE
Absolutely all receipts from ticket sales must go to The USS Arizona Memorial Fund.

Exclusive
RCA VICTOR
Recording Artist

EXCLUSIVE MANAGEMENT COL. TOM PARKER

Elvis on stage at the USS Arizona Memorial benefit.

Commission' is next in responsibility." But in the most important test of Brady's efforts, the amount of money he raised, he was failing.

Between mid-June 1958 and mid-December 1959, the eighteen months covered by the original contract, the *Arizona* Memorial fund received about $155,000 in donations. Of that amount $50,000 was from an appropriation of Hawaii's territorial legislature, and another $95,000 had been donated as the result of a broadcast of the television program "This Is Your Life." Brady had little or nothing to do with generating income from those sources. This left $10,000 at most which had come from Brady's efforts.

Yet Brady had received a 15 percent commission on *all* donations to the *Arizona* Memorial fund. Clearly, the commission was not getting its money's worth from Brady. After two short-term extensions to give Brady a chance to produce results, the commission allowed the contractual arrangement to expire at the end of July 1960. Experience had taught the commissioners to turn a deaf ear to Brady's final claim, "we are now taking a nationwide endeavor."

In terms of donations from private sources, the most significant event in the *Arizona* Memorial fundraising drive was undoubtedly the December 3, 1958, national telecast of "This Is Your Life." Hosted by television personality Ralph Edwards, each week the program centered on a different individual, usually a celebrity. The guest shared the stage with Edwards as former acquaintances spoke from off-stage about shared experiences with the guest of honor. An emotional reunion would usually follow as the acquaintance emerged after speaking.

The idea of using the show as a vehicle for the memorial fund drive first occurred to Mrs. Neil Deitrich, wife of the commandant of the Fourteenth Naval District. The idea was passed on to the PWMC by January 1958. After some deliberation the commission contacted Ralph Edwards, who agreed to use his show to promote the fundraising effort.

The December 1958 broadcast was timed to coincide as closely as possible with the anniversary of the attack. It featured, more than any one individual, the battleship USS *Arizona*. Admiral Fuqua, as senior surviving officer, stood in as the main guest. Appeals for contributions to the memorial fund were a prominent part of the program. Fuqua maintained a controlled military demeanor throughout the show, but clearly it was a time of high emotion.

The response was stunning. Contributions began to pour in immediately. During the single month from December 16 to January 15 more than $78,000 was received. In all, the commission identified more than $95,000 in donations that were attributable to the broadcast.

Even with the help of national television exposure, the PWMC realized that it would have to seek public, as well as private, funds. Since the explicit language of PL 85-344 eliminated, for the time being, the possibility of federal money, the commissioners turned to the Hawaii territorial (after August 1959, state) legislature.

In 1959 they found an ally in state Representative David McClung, a World War II Navy veteran and an ardent champion of the memorial fund drive. McClung enlisted the support of other legislators with his arguments that the *Arizona*'s dead deserved a more fitting and permanent memorial.   But the commissioners felt the need to present the legislature with a dollars-and-cents reason to appropriate state funds for the memorial.

They articulated a well-calculated appeal based on the *Arizona* Memorial's potential for Hawaii's then modest tourist industry. The commissioners knew that argument would have to be based on the rationale that the appropriation would be seed money for a developing economic base which could (and later did) become Hawaii's largest employer.

The commission canvassed key tourism executives on the memorial's potential drawing power, and all predicted that it would become an important focus of visitor interest. Prominent PWMC commissioners lobbied key legislators for an appropriation. They pursued the theme with justifications based on the memorial's certain power to stimulate "tourist interest."

The strategy worked. The legislature appropriated $50,000 in 1959. It appropriated another $50,000 in 1961 after Congressman Olin Teague of Texas pledged that

At the beginning of his long association with Hawaii, Elvis Presley raised more than ten percent of the Memorial's cost. In this 1965 photo, Elvis, right, and his manager, Col. Tom Parker, left, chat with Rear Admiral Henry S. Persons and H. Tucker Gratz, chairman, PWMC.

if the state would contribute $100,000, Congress would appropriate the funds to cover any remaining shortfall in the *Arizona* Memorial fund.

In late 1960 the memorial fund was still well short of its $500,000 goal. The editor of the Honolulu *Advertiser*, George Chaplin, volunteered to help by writing about 1,500 letters to the editors of daily papers across the nation. He asked them to help the fund drive by publishing stories or editorials about the *Arizona* Memorial project and, in turn, ask their readers to send contributions to the fund.

Among those papers which responded was the Los Angeles *Examiner*. Top popular music star Elvis Presley's manager, Colonel Tom Parker, read the *Examiner* editorial and immediately telephoned Chaplin with the offer of a Presley benefit performance in Hawaii for the *Arizona* Memorial to coincide with Presley's scheduled movie location work in Hawaii. Parker's single condition, and in this he was inflexible, was that all ticket proceeds must go directly to the memorial fund. He insisted that any overhead be covered from other sources.

Chaplin quickly referred the offer to the PWMC. The commission lost little time in accepting Parker's offer and arranged for the donation of incidental services for the concert (ticket sales, sound system, etc.). The Navy, under its authority to cooperate with the PWMC, made available its Bloch Arena at Pearl Harbor for the performance.

The March 25, 1961, concert was a sellout, with seat prices ranging from $3 to $100. The star wore a gold lamé, silver sequin lapelled sport coat and performed to the accompaniment of what one observer called "sub-navel quaking and shaking" and the screams of several thousand fans.

For the accountants, too, the show was a smashing success. When the proceeds were finally tallied, the memorial fund was $64,696.73 richer and the Memorial was lodged more permanently in the public consciousness.

A Different Approach

While the PWMC sought contributions from public and private sources, it was also confronted with a different kind of challenge—a breakaway fundraising campaign for the *Arizona* Memorial.

The commission took the position that PL 85-344 made it the sole authorized agency to solicit funds for the *Arizona* Memorial on behalf of the Navy. It was anxious to exercise total control over the effort for a number of reasons. However, the protection of the PWMC's credibility and hence its effectiveness was central to the commissioners' objections to independent campaigns. They had kept scrupulous accounts of the money passing through their hands, knowing that the campaign's chances for success could be fatally wounded by public doubts about the manner in which funds were handled. They also knew they had no control over independent fundraising groups, which might or might not keep such painstaking accounts, and if problems should arise the public would be hard pressed to distinguish between competing *Arizona* Memorial campaigns.

The full potential for conflict between the PWMC and a separate drive materialized in the person of James Roark of Phoenix, Arizona. Roark was a member of the Fleet Reserve Association (FRA), a national organization of active and retired Navy, Coast Guard, and Marine Corps personnel. He was drawn into the PWMC campaign but branched out with independent operations.

The pattern of those operations is complex and difficult to trace, but Roark led at least four different campaigns related to the USS *Arizona,* often simultaneously. First, Darrel Brady deputized Roark to head the PWMC drive for the state of Arizona sometime in 1958. Second, Roark established during the same year a private nonprofit corporation called the USS *Arizona* Memorial Foundation, Inc., for the purpose of establishing a museum in the state of Arizona to exhibit artifacts related to the battleship. Third, the governor of Arizona established a USS *Arizona* Memorial Committee, with Roark as chairman. Fourth, he also chaired the FRA's National Committee to Enshrine The USS *Arizona.*

The boundaries between these organizations and their mandates were vague and often nonexistent. From the appearance of the surviving documents, apparently he sometimes used stationery with letterheads implying nonexistent connections between the organizations. He was also negligent in presenting the accounting statements so essential to responsible fundraising work.

It was inevitable that Roark and the PWMC would come into conflict. In fact, tension arose as early as June 1958 when, upon learning of the USS *Arizona* Memorial Foundation's existence, H. Tucker Gratz objected that the foundation would "duplicate and usurp the authority and responsibility" of the PWMC. Roark replied that he intended to pursue the project regardless of the commission's objections.

Despite the uneasiness of the PWMC, Darrel Brady appointed Roark to head the commission-sanctioned fundraising drive in Arizona, an appointment which ran until January 1, 1959. The two men then devised another arrangement whereby Roark headed an FRA project in which that organization raised money for the PWMC by selling plastic model kits of the USS *Arizona.* As the PWMC representative, Brady sanctioned that project until March 31, 1959.

Roark promised to forward the proceeds to the PWMC account as they were received and to render a "final accounting of all funds received to date" before the end of each month. Neither the accounting nor the funds arrived on time. It was not until the end of May that Roark turned over to the PWMC $5,603.35 in proceeds from the Arizona state campaign. The accounting, despite repeated promises from Roark, never arrived.

More ominously, Roark was no longer content to act as a functionary of the PWMC and confine his activities to the state of Arizona. As early as January 1959 (while still a participant in the commission's Arizona state campaign) he announced that the governor would appoint a new committee, which would presumably include Roark, and that committee "will handle all matters pertaining to the USS *Arizona* both within the state *and on a national basis"* (emphasis added).

While the Memorial was under construction, the flagstaff erected in 1950 was temporarily relocated to the forward part of the sunken ship.

As it turned out, the gubernatorial committee never conducted any serious fund raising effort. But Mr. Roark was not to be sidetracked so easily. In the spring of 1959 the model kit sales campaign, which was to operate in Arizona under PWMC auspices until March 31, took on a life of its own. That life was provided by the sponsorship of the FRA's national organization, which continued the model kit program under Roark's chairmanship. This effort, with a goal of $100,000, was to be independent of the PWMC's *Arizona* Memorial fund.

It would be an understatement to say that the PWMC was upset. The spectre of confusion and damaged credibility haunted the commission. Darrel Brady, who would not receive a commission on money that went into another memorial fund, vented his anger in a cable to the PWMC:

> You have an insubordinate, opportunistic, sometimes stupid sailor
> on your hands. The authorities who have licensed, bonded and
> insured this national (Brady's) project demand he give a complete
> accounting to you and me.

The PWMC directed its expressions of alarm to the Navy, reiterating its position that Roark's efforts would "usurp the authority and responsibility" of the commission and stressing that all *Arizona* Memorial contributions should be addressed to its fund in Hawaii.

Hard at work on the Memorial structure.

The PWMC was well advised to be concerned about the Navy's attitude. Like the sorcerer's apprentice, Brady and the commission had unwittingly created a situation that had spun out of control. In this case the potential problem lay in the FRA's special relationship with the Navy. The association traditionally functioned as a quasi-official arm of the Navy, and its leaders enjoyed ready access to senior admirals. What would be the Navy's attitude toward these two campaigns, one claiming the sanction of Congress and the other possessing close and long-standing ties to the service?

On one level, at Fourteenth Naval District headquarters, the PWMC continued to enjoy Navy support. It was a support that went beyond Hawaii because the Secretary of the Navy had designated the district commandant as official liaison with the PWMC. But the FRA executed a flanking maneuver and obtained the endorsement of Admiral Arleigh Burke, Chief of Naval Operations.

This support was manifested in June 1959 when Roark's committee organized a series of premieres of the movie "John Paul Jones." The producers agreed to donate the proceeds from the premieres to the FRA drive. Called the "Governor's Premiere," Arizona Governor Paul Fanin promoted it by writing other state governors urging them to publicize the event in their areas. The key endorsement was not Fanin's, but that of Burke, who wrote in a letter the governor circulated to his colleagues, "The Fleet Reserve Association is working hard to build a memorial that will serve as an appropriate tribute to these men."

The PWMC responded swiftly. Gratz dispatched a diplomatically worded cable to Admiral Burke pointing out that PL 85-344 designated the PWMC as the official fundraising agency and, most importantly, asked the admiral to specify that all contributions should be mailed to the commission's *Arizona* Memorial fund account. In addition, Delegate John Burns asked the Secretary of the Navy to require "all groups volunteering their services on behalf of the *Arizona* Memorial to have their programs and projects approved in advance and sanctioned by the Pacific War Memorial Commission."

National officers of the Fleet Reserve Association, although supporting Roark's project, were not eager to become embroiled with the PWMC. They advised Roark to tread carefully where the commission's prerogatives were concerned and made it clear to all concerned that the FRA had no connection with Roark's nonprofit foundation.

The commission continued to press its case directly with navy officials in Washington. In November 1959 Gratz wrote Rear Admiral C.C. Kirkpatrick, Navy Chief of Information, objecting to the FRA campaign not only on the grounds of usurpation, but also because it failed to "provide proper accountability of funds." He reiterated that all donations for the *Arizona* Memorial should be sent to the PWMC's fund. Kirkpatrick's reply was cool and implicitly endorsed the FRA. He wrote that, although federal law prohibited the Navy from actively aiding any other drive, it was free to accept contributions directly from the FRA. The latter opinion directly contradicted the Navy's position of 1957, when it informed Congress that special legislation would be required before it could receive funds from the PWMC.

The question was eventually referred to the Navy Judge Advocate General, who issued an ambiguous opinion stating that "primary responsibility" for fundraising was vested by Congress with the PWMC. It stated further, "any assistance provided by the Navy to other organizations in that matter [should] be provided only upon the request or with the approval of that Commission." The opinion was silent on whether official endorsements of the Roark/FRA effort constituted "assistance."

The issue was rendered largely moot in December 1959, when the FRA presented the Navy a check for $40,000, the proceeds of its *Arizona* model kit campaign.

But even after that conclusion of the FRA drive, James Roark continued his efforts on behalf of his *Arizona* Memorial Foundation, still invoking his now-defunct connection with the PWMC. On behalf of himself and the commission, Darrel Brady wrote Roark threatening:

> If you do not cease using my name and, or, The Pacific War Memorial Commission in any connection with your present activities, letter-heads, etc., or if you attempt in any way to deceive people into

The Memorial structure was designed as a covered bridge to span—not touch—the sunken ship.

believing you hold any position or are in any way authorized by the Pacific War Memorial Commission, legal action which you so keenly deserve will be taken.

Roark persisted nonetheless, but the conclusion of the FRA campaign denied him the all important backing of that organization and the Navy. Still his activities caused concern by the PWMC and confusion in other quarters. He was particularly active in Oklahoma, where he was either vague or misleading about his connection with the PWMC. Roark also played fast and loose with data concerning the numbers of Oklahomans among the *Arizona* casualties, a matter which caused confusion among Oklahoma's Congressional delegation at the time Congress was considering the authorization of federal appropriations for the memorial.

It is difficult, if not impossible, to judge the extent to which the PWMC campaign was compromised by the competing efforts of James Roark and the FRA. Those efforts did result in raising more than $40,000 for the *Arizona* Memorial, and there is no evidence that they actually harmed the commission's fund drive. Yet there undeniably existed the potential for widespread public confusion over the split effort and poor accounting practices, so the PWMC's alarm was justifed. If this chapter in the story of the *Arizona* Memorial proves anything, it is that by the late 1950s the idea was so powerful that it could no longer be contained or monopolized by the PWMC.

A Navy boat takes the Statehood delegation to visit the Memorial. Senator E.L. Bob Bartlet, second from left.

Congressional Appropriation

T he law authorizing the construction of the *Arizona* Memorial banned the use of federal funds for the project, but the PWMC did not accept that prohibition as permanent. The commission recognized that it was an un-avoidable compromise necessary for the enactment of the law. However, the commissioners felt that once enacted, the law might be subject to amendment.

That view was expressed less than a year after the law passed when Tucker Gratz wrote Delegate Burns asking for a $150,000 appropriation for construction of the memorial. Burns refused to introduce the measure replying:

> One of the prime objections to HR 5809 was that after the bill . . . was passed by Congress, there would be a request of the Congress for the appropriation of funds. This is the usual program. Consequently, the members of Congress are inclined to view such a memorial with a jaundiced eye.

Burns went on to say that he had given his word to the skeptics that there would be no appropriation request and, "I don't want to go back on my word."

Burns' position was understandable because, as the author of HR 5809, his personal credibility was at stake. But the following year Hawaii had different representation in Congress and, as a newly admitted state, a full voting delegation in both houses. Senator Hiram Fong and Representative Olin Teague sponsored companion bills to authorize $200,000 for the memorial in the 1960 session.

But the memory of Burns' promise was too fresh. Not even Hawaii's senior Senator Oren Long could bring himself to support the appropriation. He wrote, ". . . as meritorious as this proposal may be, the original legislation . . . was predicated on assurances that the Federal Government would not be called upon to make appropriation for construction." Nor would the Navy attempt to contravene such a recent pledge. Its representative, referring to the promise of no appropriations, stated, "in view of the . . . legislative history of Public Law 85-344, the Department of the Navy is obliged to neither support nor oppose" the appropriation authorization.

Although the bills died that year, the sponsors did enlist some powerful support. The influential Senate Majority Secretary, Bobby Baker, promised his help in future efforts when he pledged, "I am a private in your army."

The following year, 1961, saw the reintroduction of Congressional proposals to authorize the use of federal funds for the construction of the *Arizona* Memorial. Hawaii's Representative Daniel Inouye submitted HR 44 to that end. Inouye's bill originally called for $200,000 but was amended to authorize $150,000 for the memorial. It cleared both houses of Congress and was signed into law as PL 87-201 on September 6, 1961.

Its passage was not trouble-free. The most important opponent was Senator Richard Russell of Georgia, chairman of the Senate Armed Services Committee. Russell's chief objection to the bill was the legacy of PL 85-344, the promise that the *Arizona* Memorial would be built without federal funds. He wrote:

> The Committee report on the original authorization indicated that there would be no cost to the government for the construction of the memorial. Because of this history, I anticipate that there will be some reluctance to approve [HR 44].

Russell was eventually won over by a strong lobbying campaign which required Joe Custer, the PWMC executive secretary, to travel to Washington. Also instrumental were the national staff of the American Veterans of World War II (AMVETS) and Bobby Baker, whose entreaties moved Vice President Lyndon Johnson to persuade his close friend Russell to allow the bill unhindered passage through his key committee.

The appropriation authorization provided for the first time an "official" definition of the memorial's purpose. According to PL 87-201 it was to "be maintained in honor and commemoration of the members of the Armed Forces of the United States who gave their lives to their country during the attack on Pearl Harbor, Hawaii, on December 7, 1941."

Visitors from around the world have paid their respects. U. Nu, the Prime Minister of Burma, examines the plaque at the flagstaff.

That sense of purpose, however, was not shared by everyone. As in the past, a wide variety of justifications were put forth for the memorial.

In 1960 Senator Fong had opined:

> The USS *Arizona* Memorial will have a dual significance to the United States, for it will not only provide appropriate tribute to the deceased men of the *Arizona* but will also stand as a national memorial to eternal vigilance against the dangers of surprise attack.

Representative Inouye echoed that theme in 1961 when he promised, "the *Arizona* Memorial will serve also as our reminder and our inspiration never again to be caught unprepared."

Other reasons were also advanced in floor discussions. Speakers stressed the rationale of treating *Arizona* as a burial site, with Inouye referring to the ship as a "common grave" for her crew. The point was elaborated on by Representative Mendel Rivers of South Carolina, who noted that the $150,000 would amount to far less than the combined military burial allowances for the entombed crewmen.

The one argument, however, made by all speakers for the bill in 1961 was that most of the funds had already been raised, turned over to the Navy, and construction actually begun. It was one thing to resist authorizing funds for a project still in its conceptual stage, but quite another to refuse funds for one which was already under way. That argument, more than any other, marked the difference between the 1961 debate and previous Congressional discussion about federal funding for the *Arizona* Memorial. That point, as Congressman Teague had promised, carried the day.

Louise (Mrs. Walter F.) Dillingham, vice chair, and H. Tucker Gratz, chairman PWMC, with Governor William Quinn, center, and artist's rendering of the Memorial, Jan. 1960.

Design, Construction, and Dedication

The design and construction of the *Arizona* Memorial were under way before the fundraising was completed. As soon as it became apparent that the money would be raised, the Navy began to draw funds from the PWMC account to begin the project.

There were many ideas for the *Arizona* Memorial design, and it is worth looking at a few of them for a notion of the variety of concepts being circulated. One writer stated that the memorial should enclose and seal the hulk of the *Arizona* to prevent the corpses of the crew from drifting loose. Another, a captain on the staff of the Commander-in-Chief Pacific Fleet, suggested that the remains be disinterred, buried at Punchbowl National Cemetery, and the battleship be dismantled, because "the general public will soon loose [sic] interest in the proposed memorial and it will gradually go into decay." A Navy public works official proposed burying the *Arizona* in a landfill extending from Ford Island and setting aside the spot as a picnic area.

Navy officials in charge of the project, however, had different ideas. Because of security and transportation requirements, they rejected the idea of incorporating any part of Ford Island in the memorial. In addition, they stipulated that the memorial was to be in the form of a bridge which would not touch any part of the sunken battleship and that it be capable of accommodating 200 people. Beyond that they imposed no design specifications.

The Navy selected the architect but leaned heavily on the PWMC for advice. That reliance was natural, for the commission had been in regular contact with members of the Hawaii chapter of the American Institute of Architects since the early 1950s. Those architects donated their services in conceptualizing design

On Memorial Day 1962, more than 300 people attended the dedication ceremony for the new USS Arizona Memorial. Many relatives of Pearl Harbor dead participated.

ideas for various PWMC projects over the years. The first money released from the *Arizona* Memorial fund was $26,000 to allow the Navy "to ascertain bids for the architectural and engineering plans for the memorial."

The selection process consisted of interviews of the prospective architects by a committee of Navy officers and Louise Dillingham, chairperson of the PWMC's design committee. The architect selected was Alfred Preis of the firm Johnson & Perkins, Preis Associates. The partnership was awarded the commission in August 1959.

Preis had actually conceived a design for a memorial at the *Arizona* site as early as 1950. He had envisioned a rock wall on the shore of Ford Island and a floating flame on the hulk of the *Arizona.*

At the 1959 selection interview Preis first submitted a design that, in his words, "confronted the physicality of the sarcophagus." Born and raised in Vienna, he had been impressed at an early age with the jewel encrusted crypts of the Hapsburg emperors and the immanent presence of death they conveyed. Preis first proposed a boat landing anchored on the *Arizona's* mooring quays which would descend to a sub-surface enclosure open to the sky and fronted with a viewing wall pierced by portholes. Visitors would be able to view the underwater remains of the ship, encrusted with the rust and marine organisms which reminded the architect of the jewelled imperial sarcophagi.

That proposal met an unenthusiastic response from the Navy; even his own partner called it "morbid." So Preis offered a second concept calling for a bridge which, in accordance with the Navy's original specifications, spanned the sunken battleship. That idea received a more positive reaction. It envisioned a catenary span over the *Arizona* and, in contrast to the first proposal, created an open and soaring effect.

He used that structural vocabulary to express his philosophical approach to the memorial's purpose. Preis viewed the United States as an essentially pacifistic nation, one which inevitably would sustain the first blow in any war. Once aroused by that shock the nation could overcome virtually any obstacle to victory. Because of that characteristic, it was unavoidable—even necessary, in Preis' view—that this nation suffer the initial defeat at Pearl Harbor. He meant his design for the memorial to be a reminder to Americans of the inevitability of sustaining the initial defeat, of the potential for victory, and the sacrifices necessary to make the painful journey from defeat to victory.

Such a complex message required a serene and noncoercive atmosphere for contemplation, so Preis designed an open assembly deck for the memorial. It would be separate from the shrine room listing the names of the *Arizona's* dead, who embodied the pain and sacrifice the architect saw as an essential element in the memorial's design.

Much has been said and written of the symbolism of two of the memorial's most striking design features: the roofline, which dips in the center and rises to peaks at either end, and the twenty-one large open spaces in the structure's sides and roof. They have been taken to represent, respectively, the low point in American fortunes in World War II eventually culminating in victory, and a continuous twenty-one gun salute to the *Arizona's* dead.

Preis feels that those interpretations are consistent with his purposes, but he incorporated those features in the design for utilitarian, rather than symbolic, purposes. The dip and peak gave the structure the proper distribution of weight for the catenary design. The large openings were included to save as much weight as possible.

The Navy began site preparation work after the PWMC released approximately $250,000 for the project in early 1960. In October the Walker-Moody Construction Company won the contract to build the memorial, which eventually cost slightly more than $500,000.

Behind the dedication ceremonies on Memorial Day 1962 lay the unsettled question of the *Arizona* Memorial's purpose. Was it primarily to entomb the dead or was it to commemorate the significance of the events of December 7, 1941?

In 1960 and 1961 that issue revolved around the question of the memorial's dedication date. A Memorial Day dedication would imply that it was essentially a cemetery; a December 7 dedication implied a commemoration of the attack. There was much confusion among officials of the PWMC and the Navy. Plans for the dedication wavered back and forth between December 7, 1961, the twentieth anniversary of the attack, and Memorial Day 1962. The latter date was chosen for the reason, as much as any other, that construction could not be completed in time for a December 7 ceremony.

One of the Arizona's bells rests on a marble pedestal in the Memorial.

Part IV: 1963–Present

Congress and the Visitor Center

The *Arizona* Memorial proved as popular as predicted. In 1963, the first full year of operation, more than 178,000 people visited the Memorial in Navy shuttle boats. The numbers rose steadily each year, and in 1968 the figure had climbed to 283,000.

The Memorial was clearly fulfilling expectations, but in a sense it was a victim of its own success. Increasing numbers of visitors were forced to wait in ever longer lines at the Navy's nondescript shuttle boat landing at the mouth of Halawa Stream. Those waits were often boring, inconvenient and exposed to inclement weather.

There was a growing feeling among those connected with the *Arizona* Memorial that improved shoreside facilities were needed, not only for visitor comfort and convenience, but also as a place to present a historical perspective on the Pearl Harbor attack. In 1967 there was a flurry of interest and a brief exchange of correspondence on the subject among senior Navy and political figures. But it was left to those on the working level in Hawaii to take the first steps forward.

That year Rear Admiral Richard Lynch, Fourteenth District Commandant, asked the PWMC for help in improving the shoreside facility. The commission responded by turning to Hawaii's Congressional delegation in January 1968, asking for appropriations to build a full-scale visitor center with a museum and theater complex. Congressman Spark Matsunaga, a former PWMC member, responded by submitting to the Navy and the commission a "discussion draft" for such a bill.

Discussion and correspondence continued during 1968. Many of the questions aired at that time came to dominate the planning and decision making for the Visitor Center in the decade that followed.

First was the issue of who should operate the museum-theater complex. In July the district commandant told the PWMC that the National Park Service (NPS) would be a more appropriate choice for the job than the Navy. The idea took the commissioners by surprise since it was the first suggestion that the Navy was considering another agency for the operation of what had been until then a strictly Navy affair.

Left: *With the Memorial as a backdrop, a model of the proposed Visitor Center is presented. U.S. Senator Spark Matsunaga, standing, addresses a group that includes, from left, Governor George Ariyoshi, state Representative Richard "Ike" Sutton, Fourteenth Naval District Commandant Rear Admiral R.S. Wentworth, Jr., former state Senator David McClung, and former state Representative Faith Evans.*

Below: *Famous surfer Duke Kahanamoku, left, became a member of the PWMC. Also pictured: Sgt. J.H. Brooks, Mrs. Leonard H. Forsberg, president, and Mrs. Butler Metzer, treasurer, Marine Corps Staff Non–Commissioned Officers Wives Club.*

The Commander-in-Chief Pacific Fleet overruled the commandant by informing the Chief of Naval Operations, "Under no circumstances should the responsibility for operation and maintenance of this Navy Memorial and its supporting facilities...be transferred to another U.S. agency..." About the same time the Office of Naval History suggested that the complex be operated as part of the Navy's museum system.

That proprietary attitude did not extend to providing Navy funds for the construction of the Visitor Center. In August 1968 the Fourteenth District Commandant submitted to Washington plans and cost estimates for a $1,400,000 museum-theater complex at the shuttle boat landing. But, he informed Congressman Matsunaga because of the demand of the Vietnam War on Navy resources, funds should be sought from private contributors and the state of Hawaii. In fact, the commandant asked the PWMC to once again assume the lead in fundraising for the proposed Visitor Center.

The Commission again looked to Hawaii's Congressional delegation for help. In January 1969 Matsunaga introduced HR 4044, the first of many such bills, to authorize an appropriation for the Navy to construct a shoreside visitor center for the *Arizona* Memorial. Despite Navy intentions to retain control of the complex, Congress clearly was thinking in terms of a National Park Service operation. House Armed Services Committee Chairman Mendel Rivers referred the bill to the Department of the Interior, the parent organization of the NPS, as well as the Pentagon, for review and comment. Matsunaga wrote that he envisioned a facility "similar in scope and purpose as [sic] the edifice at Gettysburg [National Military Park]."

The National Park Service, however, remained silent on the issue and did not respond to Rivers' request for its views. The Navy continued to look to the PWMC to raise the money. The Chief of Naval Operations wrote, "Funds for the construction of this facility will not be available through Navy programs. Continued cooperation with the Pacific War Memorial Commission in pursuit of funding is recommended." The Deputy Director of Naval History sounded the same theme when he testified before Congress to the Navy's *opposition* to HR 4044 saying erroneously, "the Pacific War Memorial Commission is taking positive steps to obtain funds for the construction of this project."

Because of the Navy's negative response, the bill made no progress and died in committee. But Matsunaga persisted and in 1971 introduced HR 206, which was similar to HR 4044. Meanwhile, in Hawaii Rear Admiral Thomas Hayward, Fourteenth Naval District Commandant and future Chief of Naval Operations, continued efforts to persuade the PWMC to conduct the fundraising drive. The commission, perhaps recalling the difficulties encountered in raising funds for the *Arizona* Memorial, declined and continued to put its faith in Congress. Harold Wright, H. Tucker Gratz's successor as chairman of the PWMC, wrote to Hayward, "it would be somewhat premature to proceed at this time with any [fundraising] plan as such action may have the effect of impeding the enactment of House Bill [sic] 206..."

Hayward's disappointment was obvious in his reply:

> Quite obviously I would support his bill completely and am willing to hold off on any lesser proposal of my own in the hopes that Congress will come up with adequate funding to do the job right. I must say, however, that I find little reason to be optimistic at the pace we are presently proceeding; nevertheless I will necessarily abide by the wishes of the Pacific War Memorial Commission.

By the end of 1971 the situation resembled the Gordian Knot. The Navy refused to support legislation which might mean a cut in other Navy programs and instead looked to the PWMC to repeat its fundraising performance of the late 1950s and early '60s. In turn, the commission declined the responsibility and looked to Congress to provide the funds. But, given the Navy's opposition to the authorization bills, mobilizing Congressional support seemed to be a hopeless task.

O.R. Greer, National President of American War Dads, places a wreath on the ship's hulk, 1948.

It was natural for Congressional sponsors to intensify the focus on the prospect of National Park Service participation in the project. In November 1971 Congressman Matsunaga explored the idea in a letter to Interior Secretary Rogers Morton noting, "existing shoreside facilities are painfully inadequate" and cited the exposure to rain and sun for waiting visitors. When the Navy opposed yet another measure for the Visitor Center in 1972 Matsunaga suggested an amendment to the bill which would allow "another Federal agency" to operate it.

He introduced HR 16201, calling for the Navy to spend $2,500,000 to build the facility, which the Park Service would subsequently operate. The Navy opposed that proposal, too, because it would draw construction funds away from other Navy programs. The Park Service broke its silence by joining the Navy in opposing the bill on similar budgetary grounds. Despite the negative reaction of the two agencies, the House passed HR 16201 in 1972.

The bombing of Pearl Harbor was investigated by the Roberts Commission shown here on Jan. 1, 1942, attending burial services.

Representative Charles Bennett of Florida, a member of the Armed Services Committee, expressed the impatience of the House with the executive agencies' reluctance to assume responsibility for construction and operation of the Visitor Center:

> If we wait around to put all the dots in the legislation, time may run out and we won't have the facility. Who gets jurisdiction 10 or 15 years from now is not very important. Right now it is going to be done this way [Navy construction]. Let's do it this way and get on with it, and 10 or 15 years from now it will be a national park.

The Senate, however, did not share that "go ahead" attitude, and the bill died in the upper house. Senator J. Strom Thurmond of South Carolina offered his opinion that "the Navy's failure to support this bill" doomed its chances.

Although his measures failed to be enacted in 1972, Congressman Matsunaga had the chance to express his frustration with the Interior Department's tardy response to Congressional requests for the agency's views. When National Park Service Acting Director Stanley Hulett finally appeared before a House Armed Services Subcommittee, Matsunaga made his point:

> ...it appears that the word [from the departmental level] has not gotten down to him [Hulett], but both in the 91st and the 92nd Congress the Department of the Interior was asked to make comments on the bill which I introduced. No reply came to the committee. Your committee, Mr. Chairman.

This bureaucratic impasse, as Thurmond had noted, was the reason the Senate declined to act. It is possible, though, that a unity of underlying purpose might have made the proponents collectively strong enough to compel the Park Service and the Navy support HR 16201. Hearings on the bill revealed widely differing views among Congressional supporters on the fundamental purpose of the memorial complex.

Admiral Chester W. Nimitz awarding medals to navy personnel aboard the USS Enterprise, Pearl Harbor, May 27, 1942. Doris Miller (beginning of line of awardees) of the USS West Virginia was the first black to receive the Navy Cross in World War II. In the background is the wreckage of battleship row.

Matsunaga himself suggested multiple purposes. He stated that the facilities would honor not only the Pearl Harbor dead, but all Americans who fought in the Pacific theater. He also declared that the complex would serve the Navy's public relations program and would inspire renewed patriotism among American visitors.

Representative Bob Casey of Texas offered his support for the bill as a means of honoring *Arizona's* dead and made no mention of other casualties. Others, despite the provisions of PL 87-201 declaring the *Arizona* Memorial a monument to *all* the American Pearl Harbor dead, shared the conviction that it memorialized only *Arizona's* dead. Hawaii's Representative Patsy Mink, who introduced legislation similar to HR 16201, testified:

> ...while the Arizona Memorial is a most fitting tribute, there is a need to pay full homage to all of the people who died during the attack, including shore-based personnel and civilians.

Spokesmen for the Pearl Harbor Survivors Association and Representative Charles Bennett seconded the theme in their statements.

Representative Charles Wilson of California echoed Matsunaga's comments on the Visitor Center as a public relations asset for the Navy and added that it would be a reminder of "our own need for national security and never to let our guard down at any time..."

Other members of Congress, such as Bennett, saw the memorial complex "not as a memorial to war but a reminder of the need for peace." Congressman Frank Annunzio of Illinois supported the measure because it would remind visitors of the "tragedy of war itself and the need for ever increasing diligence in finding ways to maintain peace and friendship among all nations." Representative Julia Butler Hansen of Washington compared the Pearl Harbor Visitor Center with the memorial at Hiroshima:

> …the Japanese have made the center of rebuilt Hiroshima a national shrine, dedicated to peace and the avoidance of further atrocities of war. Our memorial at Pearl Harbor must symbolize the same high goals for the citizens of the United States and it must be accessible to all who wish to reaffirm their commitment to those noble objectives.

The bill itself reflected a wide range of motivations. Section 2 of HR 16201 set forth its purposes as commemorating:

> …the history and American interest in the Pacific Ocean areas, and to deepen appreciation of the great heroism and patriotism of the men who lost their lives at Pearl Harbor on December 7, 1941, and in the Pacific Ocean areas during World War II.

Diversity of purpose led to confusion. That confusion is exemplified by the remarks of Representative William Dickinson of Alabama. At an August 9, 1972 hearing of the House Armed Services Committee he asked:

> Well, is this going to be a commemorative of . . . [those] buried on the *Arizona* . . . Or does this have to do with the entire World War II? What are we doing?

Although things were going poorly in Washington, there was some movement on the scene in Hawaii. Beginning about 1970, Admiral Hayward began to develop a working relationship with the senior National Park Service Representative in Hawaii, General Superintendent Robert Barrel (his title changed later to Hawaii

George S. Ishida of the United Japanese Society of Hawaii with plaque the group dedicated at the Memorial.

State Director, then Pacific Area Director). Hayward was pursuing a plan to open the waters of Pearl Harbor to civilian recreational use. He contacted Barrel for advice because of the Park Service's experience in recreational planning and management. Barrel joined a working committee that prepared a plan to develop the Aiea Bay area in a joint effort by the Navy, the NPS, and local government. Proposed recreation facilities included camping, nature trails, boating, and a new landing for the Navy's *Arizona* Memorial shuttle boats.

As a result of their contact Hayward asked Barrel informally for his views on ways the *Arizona* Memorial operation might be improved. They discussed the possibility of informal Park Service assistance and training for Navy personnel dealing with visitors. As a result of those discussions both men suggested to their respective superiors in Washington that the NPS be involved in operating the *Arizona* Memorial. Barrel also undertook to prepare a study of a possible "urban-oriented national recreation area" in Honolulu which would include the *Arizona* Memorial.

In the end, Park Service efforts on the study progressed only to the point of listing sites, including the *Arizona* Memorial, that might be included in the national recreation area. Meanwhile NPS officials recommended Congressional delay of legislative proposals to give the agency responsibility for the memorial complex, citing the lack of a completed study.

Acting Director Hulett told House Armed Services Subcommittee No. 4 that it should wait for the study before moving Matsunaga's bills. Assistant Secretary of the Interior Nathaniel Reed wrote the chairman of the Senate Armed Services Committee, "We urge delay of any further consideration of [NPS] administration [of the *Arizona* Memorial] by the Department of the Interior pending the consideration by both Departments [Navy and Interior] of potential use areas in southeast Oahu." As late as January 1973, Park Service officials in Washington took the position that legislation should await the study. But by February they recognized that the study "seems infeasible and should no longer be a factor in considering" Congressional proposals.

That retreat did not mean the end of all Park Service, much less the Navy's, objections. The 1973 session of Congress saw continued attempts to authorize the shoreside Visitor Center. Representative Matsunaga introduced several bills, and other legislators including Senator Daniel Inouye did the same.

Matsunaga's HR 746 met with Navy objections that a Navy appropriation to build the Visitor Center "might ultimately result in the elimination or reduction of funds for more vital operational facilities in the military construction program." Such objections, added to continuing NPS reservations, kept the bill mired in committee. Matsunaga relayed the gloomy news to the PWMC with the observation that the Navy's and the Park Service's "lukewarm or unfavorable reports" caused House Armed Services Committee chariman F. Edward Hebert of Louisiana to halt the bill's progress.

Even though the National Park Service no longer cited the need for further studies as a reason to delay the legislation, the agency still had reservations. Those reservations turned out to be remarkably similar to the Navy's budgetary objections.

The Navy suggested in 1973 that any legislation for the *Arizona* Memorial Visitor Center should provide that funding for both construction and operation come from the NPS budget. That proposal met with a pained reaction from Park Service officials. One of them wrote, "No consideration is given to the fact that the National Park Service also has serious financial burdens and budget restraints."

In fact, the Park Service suggested to Congress a mirror-image program which would require the Navy to operate, as well as build, the Visitor Center. The Navy, of course, refused to support the measure, noting that operation of the Center would require an additional $500,000 annually. With such a deadlock it is not surprising that the Navy considered once again the possibility of raising funds from private donors, with one officer suggesting an approach to the Retired Officers Association.

At a ceremony aboard the Memorial, a Japanese clergyman offers prayers. In the background are members of the Fleet Reserve Auxillary.

Fourteenth Naval District Study

At this point the Navy faced a pressing need to make a thorough study of the requirements for a shoreside center for the *Arizona* Memorial and to develop a strategy for building and operating that facility. To achieve that goal Rear Admiral Richard Paddock, Commandant of the Fourteenth Naval District, appointed a committee of Navy officers and civilian specialists to conduct the study in late 1973 and early 1974.

The committee studied various sites and different design and operating factors. In considering the need for the Visitor Center the committee concluded that, strictly from its perspective as an armed service, the Navy did not need the *Arizona* Memorial Visitor Center. But the members noted that the substandard facilities at the *Arizona* landing tarnished the Navy's public image and that pressure from Congress and the general public made the facility a practical necessity.

In turning to the question of which agency should run the Visitor Center once it was built, the committee considered a wide range of alternatives: the Navy, the National Park Service, the Pacific War Memorial Commission, the American Battle Monuments Commission, state and municipal government, private enterprise, and a private nonprofit corporation.

The Committee rejected the option of Navy operation on the grounds that the task was an unjustifiable departure from the service's primarily military mission. The sentimental attachment to the *Arizona* was so strong, though, that the committee felt it worthwhile to note some dissenting Navy voices in its final report. It included a proposal by an earlier commandant that the Navy retain control of the memorial structure while the Park Service operate the Visitor Center, "since the USS *Arizona* is a Navy ship and we do not want to abandon the Navy's relationship with her and her final resting place." Another Navy officer took vigorous exception to turning *any* part of the operation over to the NPS:

> ...transferring the visitor program to the Park Service will have the effect of creating an amorphous national shrine—important and meaningful but without the same sentimental attachment the Memorial has with the Navy.

Of the other possibilities considered in the study, the PWMC and the Battle Monuments Commission rejected suggestions that they might operate the visitor complex. State or municipal agencies were unsuitable because they "might open up problems in downstream areas that pertain to the security" of the naval base. Private enterprise operation was judged inappropriate for the special nature of the *Arizona* Memorial. A private nonprofit organization might, if it met strict Navy requirements, be suitable.

The most desirable option, the study concluded, was operation by the National Park Service. It gave several reasons for that conclusion:

1) Congress would probably approve, since the idea had already achieved wide circulation there in the form of authorization bills.
2) It might mean that construction funds could be taken from the NPS budget instead of the Navy's.
3) The operations would not be affected by Defense Department or Navy cutbacks.
4) National Park Service appropriations would "carry a more perpetual connotation."
5) The Park Service was "steeped in experience in control and direction of large numbers of visitors."
6) The Park Service was "steeped in experience in maintaining national parks and shrines."
7) It would continue operation of the *Arizona* Memorial "in an atmosphere of respect and dignity."
8) "No unfavorable incidents concerning the general public would reflect on the Navy's image."

Commander Howard Berc, right, presents a $9,000 check from AMVETS for the memorial wall at the Memorial to H. Tucker Gratz, left, and Congressman Olin Teague.

That position was expressed succinctly by a subsequent district commandant who wrote:

> ...we have become greatly concerned over the increasing trend in Hawaii tourism and its spillover effect on the *Arizona* Memorial Visitor program. By default the Navy at Pearl Harbor has found itself deeply involved in the tourist business, where we do not belong either by mission or experience, and we look forward to the day when the professionals from the National Park Service will take over the *Arizona* Memorial and the new visitor center...

The study committee appointed by Rear Admiral Paddock decided that the chances for a congressional appropriation funding the shoreside facility in the near future were unlikely. Since the PWMC, the most likely candidate, had already rejected a proposal to lead a fundraising drive, the Navy then turned to Branch 46 of the Fleet Reserve Association. The group was already providing financial help for improving and maintaining in the *Arizona* Memorial system. The Pearl Harbor branch of the FRA, Branch 46, was entirely separate from the earlier FRA fundraising drive which had aroused so much animosity more than a decade earlier.

The Arizona Memorial Museum Foundation

I n 1973 Branch 46 had planned a drive to raise $120,000 to improve the current *Arizona* landing. During the latter part of that year branch officers were approached by the chief civil engineering officer at Pearl Harbor. He noted the repeated failures to obtain Congressional authorization for the Visitor Center and asked them to take on the task of conducting a national campaign to raise the money from private donors. The members of Branch 46 considered the request, agreed, and in January 1974 organized the *Arizona* Memorial Museum Foundation (AMMF), a private nonprofit corporation chartered to lead the drive.

In February retired Navy Chief Petty Officer C. E. Burns, whom the Navy "generally recognized as the driving force behind the...effort," announced a goal of $6,000,000 for the AMMF campaign. But his announcement was premature, for the Navy refused to commit itself formally to the AMMF effort and told the news media that it was weighing the relative merits of the AMMF proposal, which had been solicited by a Navy spokesman, and that of another private nonprofit organization.

The competing proposal was put forth by Warren Sessler, director of the Pearl Harbor Memorial Museum (PHMM). Sessler's group proposed to build a museum in the Pearl Harbor area which would adhere to a general interpretive theme of World War II in the Pacific. The PHMM asked the Navy for the use of property adjacent to the *Arizona* Memorial landing on which to erect its museum building.

Sessler opposed the involvement of both the federal government and the AMMF in the establishment and operation of a museum at the Visitor Center. He wrote Interior Secretary Rogers Morton that the AMMF "proposes to duplicate our efforts in establishing a museum at Pearl Harbor." He objected further:

> ...ours is a private organization, and it would be a needless waste of public funds for the federal government to spend money in the operation of a museum at Pearl Harbor when this task can be performed by the Pearl Harbor Memorial Museum...

The Navy study committee examined the PHMM proposals and recommended against accepting them. The committee felt that the PHMM had not done sufficient legal groundwork and its prospects of raising the necessary funds were dim. In addition, the study observed:

> The concept of the Pearl Harbor Memorial Museum encompasses a much larger scope than that required should a museum be included as part of the *Arizona* Memorial facilities. Such a museum should be limited to a presentation of an historical record of events occurring at Pearl Harbor on December 7, 1941.

The Navy delayed for several months before coming to a final decision, a delay that caused uncertainty and tension for all involved. The frustration even included the general public. It was expressed in a Honolulu *Star-Bulletin* editorial urging the Navy, the National Park Service, the AMMF, and the PHMM to transcend their "private rivalries and a certain amount of skepticism between the parties" and propose a joint plan for the Visitor Center.

The Fourteenth Naval District broke the tension at the end of June 1974 when it publicly announced that it would endorse the AMMF fundraising drive. But that did not mean immediate action, for the proposed Navy-AMMF agreement was making its leisurely way through the Pentagon review process. Chief Burns reflected his organization's impatience and frustration with Navy channels when he pointed out, "The Navy asked the FRA to begin this project," and complained of Admiral Paddock's "wishie-washie [sic] attitudes towards our proposals."

Pearl Harbor history includes many, little–known people who became involved with community life during the war years. At a rural Hawaii school, Private First Class Conto taught physical fitness.

Finally, in December 1974 Burns and Paddock formalized the agreement by signing an eleven-point memorandum of understanding. In that document the AMMF undertook to raise $4,500,000 for the construction of the Visitor Center under conditions subject to Navy approval.

Between 1975 and 1979 the AMMF raised more than $500,000 by direct solicitation of visitors at the *Arizona* Memorial. Substantial contributions to the AMMF fund also came from the Pearl Harbor Survivors Association, the national Fleet Reserve Association and its Ladies' Auxiliary, and the Disabled American Veterans. The total also included a $350,000 appropriation from the state of Hawaii.

To obtain those state funds the legislative sponsor, Representative Faith Evans, and the AMMF had to overcome the opposition of the PWMC. The commission adhered to its position of looking to Congress, and only Congress, for financial help. For that reason it objected, without success, to the state appropriation and refused even to endorse the AMMF campaign.

Despite the obstacles the foundation raised nearly $1,000,000 during its four years of operation. That money was turned over to the Navy for the construction of the *Arizona* Memorial Visitor Center.

Transfer to the National Park Service

While the AMMF was in the midst of raising funds, the political-bureaucratic logjam in Washington began to break. Ironically, despite nearly a decade of legislative discussion, the first break occurred in the executive branch.

The Navy was anxious to transfer responsibility for the Memorial and visitor complex to the Park Service, but was at the same time reluctant to expose itself to the financial liability of constructing the Center (a feature of most of the congressional proposals). The Navy took the initiative in solving that problem with a March 12, 1975, letter from Navy Secretary William Middendorf II to Interior Secretary Rogers Morton offering to transfer the operation to the NPS "at the earliest possible date." With that strategy the Navy could begin the groundwork for the transfer without supporting legislation requiring it to spend its construction funds for the Visitor Center.

The first Interior Department response to the offer was a noncommittal acknowledgment stating that a more definitive reply would be forthcoming after a thorough Park Service review. On August 19, 1975, Acting Secretary of the Interior Kent Frizzell wrote Middendorf agreeing to the transfer "only following the appropriation of funds necessary to operate the facility at appropriate standards."

This exchange was a strictly informal statement of principle by the two departments. The Navy had no legal authority to divest itself of the responsibility, nor did the Interior Department have the authority to assume that obligation. Still, it was a start. Most importantly, it showed Congress that there was enough goodwill and agreement in principle between the two agencies to effect a successful transfer if only the right formula could be found.

That general agreement did not mean, however, that either agency was prepared to drop its opposition to the type of legislative proposal which had surfaced in Congress session after session. The Navy continued to oppose legislation that followed the formula "Navy construction, NPS operation," while the Park Service still maintained that it had too many authorized projects awaiting funding to assume immediate responsibility for the *Arizona* Memorial system. A case in point was Congressman Matsunaga's HR 1882, submitted in January, 1975. A year and a half later, still awaiting action, he wrote pessimistically to the PWMC that the bill was stalled because neither the Navy nor the NPS would support it.

Matsunaga was so discouraged that he did not even propose a fresh bill in 1977, his first year as a Senator. He wrote there was little point in repeating the exercise, since the Interior Department "has been dragging its feet in getting out a report on this." Hawaii's senior Senator, Daniel Inouye submitted S 139 in April, a bill to have the NPS accept responsibility for both construction and operation of the Visitor Center. But that measure, like others before it, failed to elicit support.

Until 1977, all attempts to authorize construction of the Visitor Center and turn it over to the National Park Service had been in the form of individual bills drafted, submitted, and considered for those specific purposes. At that point Inouye adopted a different strategy and succeeded where previous attempts had failed.

Each year Congress passed an omnibus military construction bill to authorize billions of dollars in military construction projects for the following fiscal year. Taking advantage of this, Inouye attached the Visitor Center proposal to the larger and more powerful engine—the annual military construction authorization. During the 1977 Congressional session, when the Senate considered military construction authorizations for 1978, Inouye proposed a $3,300,000 item for Navy construction of a Visitor Center complex for the *Arizona* Memorial. His Senate colleagues concurred, but the House of Representatives was reluctant to accept the authorization. The inter-house differences were reconciled in a conference

Ceremonies at the Memorial traditionally feature a volly of rifle fire by the Marine honor guard. This platform is the mooring quay where the Arizona was tied up when the Pearl Harbor attack began.

committee, which agreed to fund the project for $2,000,000. The conference committee report, adopted by both houses, included language which specified Congressional wishes that the facility be built by the Navy and operated by the National Park Service. It read, in part:

> ...prior to the award of any construction contract for the proposed *Arizona* Memorial facilities, an agreement must be executed between the Navy and the National Park Service providing that the National Park Service will assume responsibility for the operation of the memorial upon the completion of such facilities.

Senator Inouye argued for the proposal by pointing to the low level of prestige to which the U.S. armed forces had sunk in the aftermath of the Vietnam War. He maintained that an enhanced visitor facility and program at the *Arizona* Memorial would help alleviate public disdain for the military. Although Pearl Harbor was an American defeat, it was also, Inouye said, "a day of great heroism." He felt that a shoreside Visitor Center would enhance public appreciation of that heroism and thus improve the armed forces' image.

There were still members of Congress who listened to those whom Inouye called "the men of sharpened pencils." He meant the Navy officials who opposed the measure on the grounds that the project lay beyond the bounds of the Navy's mission. Inouye countered that "their mission included winning public approval of what they were doing." Why else, he asked, did the Navy budget substantial sums for recruiting advertisements, documentary films, and other public relations activities? He felt the Visitor Center would be a comparatively inexpensive way to put the Navy's best foot forward.

Pearl City in 1912. Tranquillity has returned to the islands.

This line of reasoning was not unlike some of the reasons put forth in support of HR 16201 five years before. In 1977, however, the argument was more dramatically highlighted by the historical context—public disenchantment with the armed forces in the wake of the Vietnam War.

Why did Senator Inouye's arguments succeed in 1977 when so many other efforts had fallen short? Part of the answer may lay in Inouye's influential position within the Senate's Democratic hierarchy. Years later he acknowledged that it was made plain to the Navy that continued opposition "might have distressed a few supportive members" of the Senate. Another reason might be that previous attempts, though unsuccessful in the short run, had paved the way by winning each year an increasingly wider acceptance of the need for a Visitor Center operated by the National Park Service.

The change in legislative strategy, too, undoubtedly helped. Riding piggy-back on a multi-billion dollar measure, the Visitor Center was a comparatively minor detail of a very important bill. Opponents of the program would be reluctant to jeopardize the entire construction program just to eliminate the *Arizona* Memorial Visitor Center. Finally, there was no need to solicit the views of the slow responding National Park Service in the hearings on the military construction authorization bill.

The passage of funding authorization was a signal achievement, but it was not law. The authorization language was contained in the text of the conference committee report, not the bill itself. It was the bill, minus the report, which was signed into law by President Jimmy Carter. The report served notice of Congressional intent that the Navy spend $2,000,000 to build the Visitor Center, but in the absence of Presidential concurrence it did not have the force of law.

But as a practical matter the 1975 cabinet-level exchange of correspondence between the Navy and Interior Departments went far to bridge that gap. Coupled with the language of the committee report, it provided a clear statement by both Congress and the executive branch that the National Park Service should operate the *Arizona* Memorial visitor complex.

There remained the matter of the Navy-NPS agreement required by the Congressional authorization. The transfer agreement would involve countless details concerning privileges, obligations, and logistics. It would require much time and meticulous work before such details could be agreed upon by the Navy and the Park Service. But such an agreement had to be reached before awarding the construction contract. Since construction was strictly the Navy's responsibility, it made little sense to have the process delayed by the time-consuming negotiations dealing with post-construction operation.

That problem was solved in early 1978, when representatives of the Navy and the NPS signed a letter of agreement in which the Navy promised to transfer, and the Park Service agreed to accept, responsibility for operating the Memorial and Visitor Center. The letter acknowledged that the details would be worked out later in support and use agreements between the agencies.

The way was now clear for work to begin. Accepting a design for the museum-theater visitor complex submitted by the architectural firm of Chapman, Cobeen, Desai, Sakata, Inc., the Navy awarded the construction contract to S & M Sakamoto. Ground was broken for the project on October 19, 1978. The $2,000,000 authorization and the approximately $1,000,000 from the AMMF proved inadequate for the center's eventual $4,900,000 price tag, but the Navy made up the difference from savings on other projects and funds not encumbered for specific purposes.

Aware that, although the Visitor Center would be a Navy construction project, it would be operated by the National Park Service, the Navy deferred to Robert Barrel and other NPS officials in functional planning of the Visitor Center. The Navy's district civil engineer wrote Barrel in May 1977:

> In view of the National Park Service's role as ultimately having...responsibility for the permanent shoreside facilities, your input regarding National Park Service facilities' criteria is requested as soon as possible.

Souvenir of your Pearl Harbor Cruise aboard the "Adventure"

Postcard souvenir from one of the private tour boats that began operating soon after the war ended. Visitors were taken as close to the Arizona's wreckage as allowed by the Navy. Today, the National Park Service administers a permanent visitor facility.

Responding to that invitation, Barrel designed the complex's visitor flow pattern taking visitors first to a front desk where they would be issued a program ticket. With the announcement of their program number visitors would then go to one of the two theaters for a twenty-minute film and a short talk by a park ranger. Then visitors would exit the theater and board a Navy shuttle boat for a round trip to the *Arizona* Memorial.

Barrel was aware that the system had a variable but finite capacity, depending on the intervals between programs, shuttle boat speeds, and other factors. He knew also that between 1963 and 1976 the annual number of people visiting the *Arizona* Memorial by Navy shuttle boat had increased from 178,872 to 585,953—a rise of 300 percent. If that rate of increase continued, and there was no indication it would not, it would be only a matter of time before the Memorial-Visitor Center system faced more visitors than it could accommodate.

Barrel confronted the problem and decided *not* to attempt to design a system with an infinitely expandable capacity. He accepted the fact that, in order to preserve the quality of visitor experience, some people would not be accommodated. The system's finite carrying capacity was a fundamental precept in NPS planning for the Visitor Center.

Concurrent with the basic planning, NPS administrators worked with the Navy and other agencies to lay the groundwork for the operation of the Visitor Center. In 1979 the AMMF changed its name to the *Arizona* Memorial Museum Association and became a nonprofit cooperating association that would operate a bookstore at the Visitor Center. Proceeds would be used to support the Park Service's interpretive programs.

On March 21, 1980, the Navy and the NPS executed a use agreement formally permitting the Park Service to manage the Visitor Center and adjacent grounds which lay on Navy property. On September 10, representatives of the two agencies signed a support agreement spelling out in detail what services would be supplied by the Navy, which would be reimbursable, and which would be free.

On October 10, 1980, in a ceremony reminiscent of the 1962 dedication of the Memorial, the Navy turned the Visitor Center and operation of the *Arizona* Memorial over to the National Park Service. That act closed a major chapter in the history of the *Arizona* Memorial. It also heralded the advent of a new era in which the Park Service would provide professional management for one of Hawaii's most important visitor attractions.

Challenges For the Future

The professional expertise of the National Park Service is sure to be challenged in the years to come by the persistence of old problems and changing conditions. The principal questions looming in the foreseeable future bear striking resemblance to issues that have surrounded the *Arizona* Memorial and Visitor Center from their inception.

The most immediately pressing and obvious of those issues is the increasing number of visitors. The unrelenting rise in numbers which first prompted the need for the Visitor Center continues unabated. In 1981, the first full year of operation, 851,320 people visited the complex and Memorial, and in 1982 there were a record 1,039,024 visitors. There is every indication that the totals for subsequent years will be even greater. On especially busy days the NPS staff may turn away more than 2,000 visitors because program capacity is unequal to the demand.

The Park Service can make and has made adjustments to accommodate the flood. Theater capacity was increased by more than 10 percent in 1982, as was shuttle boat capacity and speed. The NPS has experimented with shortening the intervals between programs. It might be possible to increase the number of hours per week of operation.

These changes undoubtedly allow, or would allow, the *Arizona* Memorial Visitor Center to accommodate thousands of people who otherwise would be turned away. They do, however, have a price. Compressing program intervals, stretching staffing resources, and packing increasing numbers into each program will, in the long run, dilute the quality of each visitor's experience.

The designers of the system's components chose to impose limits. In designing the interpretive program Robert Barrel consciously accepted three premises: 1) a certain standard of program quality must be maintained; 2) maintaining that standard depends on respecting the finite capacity of the system and the site; and 3) visitors beyond that limit should be turned away rather than compromise quality standards. When Alfred Preis designed the Memorial, he saw the opportunity for contemplation as essential to drawing the full meaning and significance from the site.

Just how crowded and rushed can the NPS allow visitation on the Memorial to become before the experience becomes just another meaningless stop on the tourist agenda? Should the Park Service draw a line beyond which it will not compromise the quality of its interpretive program? If so, where should that line be?

The question of how best to reconcile the competing demands of popularity and quality standards is a continuing one, and the solution most likely will be reached gradually through experimentation. Unfortunately, the ambiguous legal status of the *Arizona* Memorial and Visitor Center may prove to be a more serious problem for the National Park Service.

Both are located on Navy property in the midst of an important military base. The Memorial and Visitor Center are unique, or nearly so, among U.S. National Park Service operations in that there exists no authorizing legislation defining the facility's boundaries and definitively establishing it as an NPS-administered site.

The language of the interdepartmental executive agreements and the conference report of the 1978 military construction authorization act are adequate for the day-to-day relationship between the Navy and the Park Service. But, as noted earlier, they are not law.

There are many reasons why a firmer legal cornerstone might be needed. Navy officers have often expressed a proprietary attitude toward the *Arizona* Memorial. It is not beyond the realm of possibility that someday a prominent Navy personality would launch a drive to "return the *Arizona*" and its Visitor Center to the Navy. Such a campaign might fly in the face of budgetary and political reality, but an emotionally motivated campaign might be willing to confront those obstacles. Or, operating more indirectly, it might take the form of quasi-official groups and/or the general public making the same demand.

At least as likely is the prospect of a pressing Navy need, or the perception of such a need, to reclaim control of the Memorial or the Visitor Center site for security or operational reasons. There always exists the possibility of war, a major military buildup at Pearl Harbor, or the construction of a sensitive installation

In the early days, fewer visitors made it possible for the Navy to administer the Memorial. Today, crowds of visitors challenge the resources of the National Park Service, but the Navy still operates the shuttle boat fleet.

nearby. In such an event Navy officials might review the status of the Memorial and Park Service operations with an eye toward exerting more direct control or even eliminating the visitor program entirely.

Admittedly, enabling legislation would be flimsy protection against military exigencies, real or imagined. During World War II the armed forces invoked military necessity to take over the use of a number of national parks despite the existence of legislation protecting those areas. But the passage of enabling legislation would compel the Navy to make a solid case for terminating the NPS program. At the worst it would provide the Park Service with a legal foundation to recover the Memorial and Visitor Center after any military need for the site had passed.

Also, for reasons entirely unrelated to its relationship with the Navy, the *Arizona* Memorial Visitor Center might need more definitive legislation. If Park Service budget cuts ever become so severe that NPS activity at one or more sites has to be reduced or even terminated, then ambiguous legal authorization might well be among the criteria used to select candidates for a drastic cut.

These are admittedly far-fetched possibilities. Yet the fact remains that there is limitless potential for confusion, dispute, and disaster arising from the lack of a clear law establishing the *Arizona* Memorial and Visitor Center as an NPS site. Clearly, the last chapter in the long history of Congressional deliberation on this matter has yet to be written.

The most abstract challenge facing the National Park Service, and in many ways the most difficult to come to grips with, is the continuous question of the meaning of the *Arizona* Memorial. In past public discussions, proponents have expounded on a wide variety of themes to define its purpose. The "official" purpose put forth in PL 87-201 notwithstanding, there remains an enormous diversity of individual interpretations.

The NPS visitor program does not really confront the issue of the Memorial's purpose and for good reason. There are potentially as many purposes as there are individual visitors. Some view it as a reminder that America should be eternally vigilant and never again be caught unprepared by the outbreak of war. Others see it as evidence of the tragic price of war, a monument to the need to seek peaceful solutions to international differences.

Many, especially those of the generation that played an active role in World War II, view the *Arizona* Memorial as a proud tribute to American ability to achieve a great victory after facing initial disadvantage. For others of that generation, a visit to the *Arizona* Memorial rekindles the passions of that period, reawakening a hatred of Japanese, exacerbated by current economic tensions. Still other Americans are moved by a stirring of patriotism ranging in tone from xenophobia to simple love of country.

Despite the attack, the West Virginia's ensign continued to fly.

Nor is the commemoration of the dead overlooked. Visitors are certainly reminded of the *Arizona's* casualties. Others remember all who were killed in the December 7, 1941, attack. And some think of those killed in other battles and other wars.

Younger visitors, who have no personal recollection of World War II, usually take a more detached view of the Memorial and its meaning. For many it is a history lesson, an intellectual experience rather than an emotional one. Others take to heart the various meanings older visitors ascribe to the Memorial.

Foreign visitors may invest the Memorial with entirely different meanings. Those from nations allied with the United States in World War II may see the program's content as slighting their nations' contribution to the common victory. They may feel that their own countries also suffered greatly during the war and that the visitor program should give equal attention to the casualties of all nations which fought in the Second World War.

And what goes through the minds of Japanese visitors, who comprise an increasing share of the visitor total? Some experience a sense of pride when they visit the site of one of their nation's most spectacular military triumphs. Disconcerting as that thought may be to Americans, it must be remembered that the Japanese government presented the Pearl Harbor attack to its subjects as a David and Goliath victory—an event to swell every Japanese heart with pride. For other Japanese a visit to Pearl Harbor is the occasion for bitter regret over the recklessness of the Japanese government in setting their nation on the road to disaster and indescribable suffering. Younger Japanese, like younger Americans, may have only the vaguest notions of World War II.

Obviously, then, there can be no single meaning or significance applicable to all visitors to the *Arizona* Memorial. Regardless of how many "official" statements of purpose are promulgated, each visitor will approach the experience with and be guided by his or her personal predisposition. It is not possible to be all things to all people. The National Park Service can not expect to impose to single meaning on the visitor program. Rather, it faces the challenge of presenting the story of the Pearl Harbor attack in a way that transcends the wide range of personal opinions while respecting the right of each person to hold his or her personal views.

Then perhaps we can move toward a vantage point which, in the words of one historian:

> … takes no comfort in scapegoats and offers no sanctuaries for private or national claims of moral righteousness, but rather admits that as two nations are drawn into violent conflict, something very tragic in human affairs is taking place.

Photo and Illustration Credits

Art and Illustration

Front Cover: *Day of Infamy* by Kipp Soldwedel, 1969
Page 1: Diagrams by Ron Rubenstein based on historical sources
Page 10: *Cease Present Exercise* by Arthur Beaumont, 1938
Page 16: *Admiral Isoroku Yamamoto* by Shugaku Homma, 1943
Pages 48, 54: Drawings by Jerry L. Livingston
Page 109: *Admiral Nimitz* by Albert K. Murray.
Page 112: Diagram by Ron Rubenstein

Photography

Arizona Memorial Museum Association: 54-55 (Drawings by Jerry L. Livingston).
Army Museum Hawaii: 42 top; 59 top.
Bishop Museum: 11, 14 top; 15 (Tai Sing Loo); 71 (Baron Goto); 90 (R.J. Baker).
Camera Hawaii: 40 top; 80 (Werner Stoy); 89; 103 (Walter Immekus); 112 (Werner Stoy); back flap.
Maxine Cass: 7
David Cornwell: Inside back cover.
Defense Audiovisual Agency: 27 bottom; 32 top; 38 bottom; 39; 41 top left; 42 bottom; 43 top.
N.R. Farbman, LIFE Magazine @ 1956, Time, Inc.; 8.
H. Tucker Gratz: 65
Hawaii State Archives: Inside front cover; 12, 13; 14 bottom; 19; 20; 22; 23 top; 24 bottom; 25 bottom left; 26; 27 (Tai Sing Loo); 33 top; 35 top; 47; 56-57 (PWMC Collection); 61; 63 (PWMC Collection); 64; 67; 68; 69; 72; 77; 85 (PWMC Collection); 93; 94.
Hawaii Visitor's Bureau: 9.
Paul Henning: Front flap; 5; 6; 97; 98; 99; 100; 101; 102; 105; 106; 107; 108; 109 bottom; 110; 111; back cover.
Mark Hertig: 52 top.
Richard Hilgendorf: 104.
Honolulu Star-Bulletin: inset 8; 73; 76; 79; 82; 83.
Light, Inc: 101 top.
Dan Martinez: 81, 109
National Archives: 34 top; 45.
National Park Service: 18 top; 21 bottom; 22; 23 bottom; 37 top; 49; 50; 51.
Naval Historical center: 10; 18 bottom; 41 top right/bottom.
U.S. Navy: 16; 21 top; 28 (courtesy Richard Wisniewski); 29; 31 top; 38 top; 75 (John Greenwood).
Allan Seiden: 4; 53.
Ship Lore, Ltd.: Front Cover.
University of Hawaii Archives: 24 top; 25 top/lower right; 27 top left; 30; 31 bottom; 32 bottom; 33 bottom; 34 bottom; 35 bottom; 36; 37 bottom; 40 bottom; 43 bottom; 46; 59 bottom; 87.
R.P. Wilcox: 2.

Appendix, Sources, and Notes

Appendix A: Public Law 85–344

March 15, 1958
[H.R. 5809]

AN ACT To authorize construction of a United States Ship Arizona Memorial at Pearl Harbor.

Be it enacted by the Senate and House of Representatives of the United States of America in Congress assembled, That the Secretary of the Navy may—

(1) accept contributions for the construction of a memorial and museum to be located on the hulk of the United States ship Arizona or adjacent United States property in Pearl Harbor, Territory of Hawaii;

(2) authorize Navy activities to furnish material to the Pacific War Memorial Commission for use in national promotion of a public subscription campaign to raise funds for a United States Ship Arizona Memorial;

(3) authorize Navy activities to assist in conceiving a design and in determining the construction cost for the memorial;

(4) undertake construction of the memorial and museum when sufficient funds have been subscribed for completion of the structure; and

(5) provide for maintenance of the memorial and museum when completed.

Approved March 15, 1958.

Appendix B: Public Law 87–201

September 6, 1961
[H.R. 44]

AN ACT To authorize the appropriation of $150,000 for use toward the construction of a United States Pacific War Memorial.

Be it enacted by the Senate and House of Representatives of the United States of America in Congress assembled, That the Act entitled "An Act to authorize construction of a United States Ship Arizona Memorial at Pearl Harbor", approved March 15, 1958 (Public Law 85–344; 72 Stat. 36), is hereby amended by adding at the end thereof the following:

"SEC. 2. There is hereby authorized to be appropriated to the Secretary of the Navy, for use toward the construction of such memorial and museum, the sum of $150,000.

"SEC. 3. Such memorial and museum shall be maintained in honor and in commemoration of the members of the Armed Forces of the United States who gave their lives to their country during the attack on Pearl Harbor, Hawaii, on December 7, 1941."

Approved September 6, 1961.

Appendix C: Visitor Center Appropriation

HOUSE OF REPRESENTATIVES
95TH CONGRESS
1st Session

REPORT No. 95–494

MILITARY CONSTRUCTION AUTHORIZATION ACT, 1978
July 12, 1977.—Ordered to be printed

Mr. NEDZI, from the committee of conference, submitted the following
CONFERENCE REPORT
[To accompany S. 1474]

PEARL HARBOR NAVAL STATION, HAWAII—ARIZONA MEMORIAL

In its bill, the Senate added $3.3 million for visitor facilities at the ARIZONA Memorial, Pearl Harbor, Hawaii. House conferees expressed reservations about providing authority under the Military Construction Authorization Act for the construction of memorial facilities and questioned the scope of the proposed project. The House conferees were of the opinion that $2.0 million should be sufficient to provide suitable facilities for the memorial. After a thorough review of the history of this project, the conferees agreed to authorized $2.0 million.

Further, the conferees agreed that prior to the award of any construction contract for the proposed ARIZONA Memorial facilities, an agreement must be executed between the Navy and the National Park Service providing that the National Park Service will assume the responsibility for the operation of the memorial upon completion of such facilities.

National Park Service Ranger addresses audience in the visitor center theatre.

Appendix D: Transfer Proposal

DEPARTMENT OF THE NAVY
OFFICE OF THE SECRETARY
WASHINGTON, D.C. 20350

March 12, 1975

The Honorable Rogers C.B. Morton
The Secretary of the Interior
Department of the Interior
Washington, D.C. 20240

Dear (Mr. Secretary) Rog,

I am writing in the belief that our respective departments should have a compatible objective for the eventual disposition of the United States Ship Arizona Memorial in Pearl Harbor. My staff has met with representatives of the National Park Service on this subject. I understant that, in principle, and without commitment as to timing, they are in basic agreement.

The Navy is concerned that the number of visitors desiring to tour the Memorial has outstripped the capacity of facilities for their accommodation. There is now insufficient parking, boat capacity, and on-shore reception area. More than 500,000 persons visited the Memorial in 1973. The number is increasing on a trend of 18 percent a year.

We have completed a study of necessary improvements of facilities, and the associated investment and annual operating costs. Quite frankly, I cannot foresee that Navy appropriations will ever be adequate to support the reasonable convenience and necessity demands of public visitors. While I regret that prospect, I respect the judgement that Navy should not divert funds from a military readiness mission, to tourist support.

I propose that we agree on the objective of transfer of the Memorial to your Department, at the earliest date that you consider resources of your Department adequate for its care and operation. On our part the Navy will support such legislation for that purpose as may be agreeable to the Department of the Interior, and is prepared to fully cooperate with your Department to ensure that current Navy management of the Memorial is consistent with your longer term planning. In that regard we would prefer to commence procurement of new boats and to carry on the boat transportation function in a manner fully compatible with your overall management of the Memorial operation.

Navy would like to offer, for your affirmation, Navy participation in a consultative role in development of your plans for improvements, displays and exhibits at the Memorial, and an understanding that the naval character of the Memorial will be preserved.

Sincerely,
/S/Bill
J. William Middendorf II
Secretary of the Navy

Appendix E: Transfer Acceptance

United States Department of the Interior

OFFICE OF THE SECRETARY
WASHINGTON, D.C. 20240

AUG 19 1975

In Reply Refer To:
L58–LL
ES–13897

Honorable J. William Middendorf II
Secretary of the Navy
Washington, D.C.

Dear Mr. Secretary:

We are pleased to respond further to your letter of March 12 proposing a transfer of the U.S.S. "Arizona" Memorial to the Department of the Interior. We have had an opportunity to consider the views of the National Park Service and the recommendation of the Advisory Board on National Parks, Historic Sites, Buildings, and Monuments on the proposal.

We concur with the statement that you have made in the next to the last paragraph of your March 12 letter that the "Arizona" Memorial be transferred to this Department at the earliest date that resources are availalbe for its care and operation. We appreciate the Navy's concern for the perpetuation of this memorial and that such related interpretive services are diversions from the Navy's military readiness mission.

Seal of the Pearl Harbor Survivors Association. As part of the Park Service's interpretive program, members of the Association frequently speak at the Visitor Center.

The National Park Service believes that it would be appropriate to include the memorial and the shoreside facilities as a part of the National Park System. The Advisory Board has recommended that the Service conduct a feasibility study. Accordingly, the Service will program a study for fiscal year 1977. This study will develop cost estimates and other data for a Departmental recommendation on legislation to implement the transfer. The study will be under the direction of the National Park Service Western Region Director, whose address is Western Region Office, National Park Service, 450 Golden Gate Avenue, Box 36036, San Francisco, California 94102, and telephone number is 415-556-4196. Navy participation in the study will be welcome.

Owing to the fiscal constraints applicable to both our Departments, it is our intention to recommend legislation which would provide for a transfer only following the appropriation of funds necessary to operate the facility at appropriate standards.

We appreciate very much your interest and the cooperation of the Navy staff in this matter.

Sincerely yours,
/S/ Kent Frizzell
Kent Frizzell
Acting Secretary of the Interior

Sources

This study is based primarily on documentary evidence found in the files of organizations and agencies which played important roles in the history of the USS *Arizona* Memorial and Visitor Center. The most significant documentation is in the files of the Pacific War Memorial Commission, now in the Hawaii State Archives in Honolulu. The commission was instrumental in bringing the Memorial into existence, and it was frequently consulted by the Navy on subsequent issues relating to the Memorial (such as the establishment of the Visitor Center).

Another important source was the files of the National Park Service's Pacific Area Office in Honolulu. They contain material relating to the role of the Park Service in Hawaii during the transfer period. Important documents shedding light on the legislative process in Congress are also in these files.

The holdings of the Navy's Pearl Harbor command (COMNAVBASE) were digested in the form of a volume entitled *Arizona Memorial Shoreside Facility Study* (AMSFS). That study, available from the Public Affairs Office at Pearl Harbor, includes important documents reproduced in its numerous appendixes. Completed in 1974, the study also has miscellaneous documents loosely attached to the pages of the volume. These miscellaneous documents are on file with the AMSFS at the Public Affairs Office, and, when cited in the Notes, they are indicated by the words, "filed with AMSFS." Additional Navy documents are in the files of OICC, Mid–Pacific at Pearl Harbor.

Other sources consulted include daily newspapers, the files of the *Arizona* Memorial Museum Foundation (now in custody of Branch 46, Fleet Reserve Association at Pearl Harbor), the files of the Fleet Reserve Association's national headquarters in Washington, Congressional documents, the Operational Archives of the U.S. Naval Historical Center, and the personal files of the late David McClung.

Written records were supplemented by personal interviews with Robert Barrel, Gary Beito, George Chaplin, Faith Evans, H. Tucker Gratz, Senator Daniel Inouye, Senator Spark Matsunaga, the late David McClung, and Alfred Preis. C.E. Burns Provided additional information in a personal communication.

This plaque on Ford Island marks the spot where the Tennessee and the West Virginia were tied up at the time of the attack.

Notes

The following abbreviations are used throughout:

Adv   Honolulu *Advertiser*
AMMF   Files of the *Arizona* Memorial Museum Foundation
AMSFS   The Fourteenth Naval District's *Arizona Memorial Shoreside Facility Study*
FRA   Files of the Fleet Reserve Association's national headquarters
PAAR   Files of the National Park Service's Pacific Area Office
PWMC   The Pacific War Memorial Commission record group in the Hawaii State Archives
SB   Honolulu *Star-Bulletin*

Part I: Before the Attack

The USS Arizona, Ship of Destiny

p. 14   *the same year.* Technical data from Norman Friedman, Arthur D. Baker III, Arnold S. Lott, and Robert F. Sumrall, *USS Arizona (BB 39)* (Annapolis: Leeward Publications, 1978), *passim.*

17   *raised and repaired.* Commandant, Navy Yard, Pearl Harbor to The Vice Chief of Naval Operations, 25 July 1942, *Arizona* Loss File, Operational Archives, U.S. Naval History Division, Washington, D.C.

17   *surrender in 1945.* Emmanuel Raymond Lewis, *Seacoast Fortifications of the United States: An Introductory History* (Annapolis: Leeward Publications, 1979), 123.

Part II: 1941–1954

Remembering Pearl Harbor

29   *inscribed on its walls.* "Assistant Navy Chief Commends Tony Todaro On War Memorial Plan", *SB* July 22, 1944, p. 7. "Chief War Memorials That Have Been Proposed and Considered", undated, PWMC.

29   *plaques in the memorial.* "PH Memorial Design Proposed Here For Erection in Capital", *Adv,* April 26, 1944, p. 2.

29   *built in Hawaii.* "PH Memorial Group Elects New Trustees", *SB*, August 2, 1944, p. 7.

The Pacific War Memorial Commission

44   *accrue to Hawaii.* Midkiff to Gratz, Dec. 1, 1950, PWMC.

44   *"system that is desired."* Honolulu Planning Commission Minutes, Feb. 18, 1952, PWMC.

44   *"rehabilitating" the Arizona.* "Work Begun to Preserve Hulk of USS Arizona", *Adv,* Oct. 10, 1950, pp. 1, 4. "2 Plaques Honor PH War Dead", *Adv,* Dec. 12, 1950, pp. 1, 8. "1960–61 Minutes" file, PWMC.

National Interest

46   *"and Hickam Field."* "Lest We Forget . . . ", *Collier's,* July 22, 1950, p. 74.

46   *"hope on earth."* U.S. Congress. *Congressional Record,* Vol. 96, Part 10, pp. 14034-35, Aug. 31, 1950. "Highlights of the USS Arizona Story", *Pacific War Memorial System* (PWMC newsletter), Vol. I, No. 1, p. 3, PWMC. Amvets Administrator to Gratz, June 6, 1952, PWMC.

46   *"commemorating Pearl Harbor Day."* Solomenson to Cross, Oct. 2, 1952, PWMC.

47   *could not visit.* "Plans for Memorial on Hulk of Arizona Face Big Obstacles", *SB*, Aug. 8, 1950, p. 5.

47   *a shameful defeat.* "Lest We Forget . . . ", *op. cit.*

47   *"day of infamy."* Short to Gratz, Nov. 26, 1952, PWMC.

47   *"uncalled for."* Minutes, Nov. 4, 1954, PWMC.

Part III: 1955–1962

Navy Overtures

57   *"within her hull."* COMFOURTEEN to Secretary of the Navy, Nov. 23, 1955, PWMC.

57   *honorary chairman of the PWMC.* Burke endorsement cited in Gratz to North, Aug. 27, 1957, PWMC. Nimitz endorsement in Minutes, July 12, 1956, PWMC.

57   *PWMC participate, too?* Minutes, March 29, 1956, PWMC.

57   *work with that organization.* "Navy Chief Urges Shrine Over Arizona", *Adv,* May 12, 1956, p. A–6. "Navy Club, Memorial Group To Sponsor Arizona Shrine", *Adv,* May 14, 1956, p. 7.

57   *funds for an Arizona Memorial.* PWMC minutes of Dec. 7, 1959, refer to an Aug. 3, 1956, meeting at which the commandant made the proposal.

58   *to Bishop Trust.* Minutes, July 11, 1957, PWMC.

Dedication plaque placed at the base of the flagstaff on temporary Memorial platform by Admiral Arthur Radford.

Authorizing Legislation

p. 58 *"our own community families."* U.S. Congress. *Congressional Record,* Vol. 103, Part 12, p. 15634, Aug. 22, 1957.

58 *"to a successful conclusion."* Pate to Roark, Oct. 31, 1958, PWMC.

58 *"a suitable resting place"* Fuqua to Roark, Nov. 21, 1958, PWMC.

58 *"cannot be recovered from the hull."* Both men used identical wording in separate documents. Gratz, undated [1957] statement, PWMC. Stephan quoted in U.S. Congress, 85th Congress, 2nd Session, Senate Report No. 1229 (Jan. 28, 1958).

60 *"Arizona to reoccur."* Burke to Roark, Oct. 24, 1958, PWMC.

60 *found in strength.* U.S. Congress. *Congressional Record,* Vol. 104, Part 3, p. 3225, March 3, 1958.

60 *"great defeat for us."* Nimitz to Gratz (holograph), July 11, 1961, PWMC.

60 *"Memorial at Pearl Harbor."* U.S. Congress, 85th Congress, 1st Session. HR 5801.

60 *"amending it to death."* U.S. Congress. *Congressional Record,* Vol. 104, Part 3, pp. 3224–27, March. 3, 1958.

Fundraising

62 *all operating expenses.* Brady–PWMC Agreement, June 16, 1958; Supplementary agreement, Oct. 20, 1959 and April 7, 1960, PWMC.

62 *cost for the Memorial.* Minutes, June 25, 1956, PWMC.

62 *"a more modest $500,000."* Custer to Brady, March 26, 1958, PWMC.

62 *"commission and the campaign."* Miki to Peal, April 7, 1960, PWMC.

62 *Brady had been involved.* Custer to Brady, Feb. 6, 1959, PWMC.

62 *"nothing definite lined up."* Handwritten "Memo to the file", undated [1960], PWMC.

62 *"nebulous promises."* Styne, "Memo to the file", June 4, 1960, PWMC.

64 *"next in responsibility."* Brady to Gratz, Aug. 7, 1959, PWMC.

64 *"This Is Your Life."* Custer to Ramelb, May 4, 1960, PWMC.

64 *"a nationwide endeavor."* Brady to Gratz, May 17, 1960, PWMC.

64 *promote the fundraising effort.* Custer to Deitrich, Jan. 22, 1958; Minutes, May 9, 1958, PWMC.

64 *attributable to the broadcast.* Custer to PWMC, Jan. 8, 1960; Minutes, Dec. 18, 1959, PWMC.

64 *fitting and permanent memorial.* David McClung, interview with author, Honolulu, Sept. 13, 1982.

64 *Hawaii's largest employer.* Gratz to Burns, March 6, 1959, PWMC.

64 *"tourist interest."* PWMC to McClung, March 16, 1959; Mirikitani to Gratz, April 28, 1961; Gratz and Dillingham to members of State House and Senate Capital Improvement Committees, May 24, 1961; Miyake to Gratz, April 26, 1961, PWMC.

65 *shortfall in the Arizona Memorial fund.* The 1959 sum was from McClung's "pork barrel", a custom which allowed each legislator discretion to include projects for his or her district in the state budget. Additionally, the 1959 legislature authorized a $77,000 bond issue for the *Arizona* Memorial, but technicalities in Hawaii's statehood legislation invalidated the authorization. David McClung, interview with author, Honolulu, Sept. 13, 1982.

65 *contributions to the fund.* Chaplin to "My Dear Fellow Editor," Nov. 25, 1960, PWMC.

65 *from other sources.* Chaplin to Gratz, Dec. 7, 1960; Chaplin to Townes, Jan. 18, 1961, PWMC. George Chaplin, interview with author, Honolulu, Sept. 13, 1982.

65 *several thousand fans.* Mayer, Phil. "Elvis Sings Up A Storm to Aid Arizona Memorial", *SB,* March 26, 1961, p. 1.

65 *$64,696.73 richer.* Gratz note to file, March 29, 1961; Bishop Trust Co. statement, April 30, 1961, PWMC.

A Different Approach

66 *Committee to Enshrine The USS Arizona Memorial.* Brady to Custer, Aug. 16, 1958; Gratz to Solomons, June 4, 1958; State of Arizona Certificate of Incorporation for USS *Arizona* Memorial Foundation, Inc., Dec. 7, 1959; McFarland to Quinn, Nov. 21, 1958; Roark to Gratz, Jan. 16, 1959, PWMC.

66 *between the organizations.* Roark to Quinn, Sept. 11, 1959, PWMC.

Basalt stone on Ford Island with plaque dedicated by the Navy Club in 1955—the first permanent Pearl Harbor memorial.

66   *"authority and responsibility" of the PWMC.* Gratz to Solomons, June 4, 1958, PWMC.

66   *the commission's objections* Roark to Gratz, June 27, 1958, PWMC.

66   *until March 31, 1959.* Brady to PWMC, cablegram May 31, 1959, PWMC.

66   *never arrived.* Roark to Gratz, Jan. 16, 1959; Gratz to Solomons, Dec. 11, 1959; Gratz to Brady, July 27, 1959; Brady to Roark, March 11, 1959; Gratz to Roark, Feb. 17, 1961; "Digest of Meeting With Roark", undated, PWMC.

66   *"on a national basis"* Roark to Gratz, Jan. 16, 1959, PWMC.

67   *the PWMC's Arizona Memorial Fund.* Roark to Quinn, Sept. 11, 1959, PWMC.

67   *"accounting to you and me."* Brady to PWMC, cablegram May 31, 1959, PWMC.

67   *its fund in Hawaii.* Gratz to Solomons, June 4, 1959, PWMC.

68   *"tribute to these men."* Burk to Fanin, June 17, 1959, PWMC.

68   *Arizona Memorial fund account.* Gratz to Burke, cablegram July 7, 1959, PWMC.

68   *"sanctioned by the Pacific War Memorial Commission."* Burns to Franke, July 3, 1959, PWMC.

68   *Roark's nonprofit foundation.* Langdon to Roark, June 16, 1959, FRA.

68   *should be sent to the PWMC's fund.* Gratz to Kirkpatrick, Nov. 23, 1959, PWMC.

68   *directly from the FRA.* Kirkpatrick to Gratz, Dec. 24, 1959, PWMC.

68   *receive funds from the PWMC.* Stephan to Vinson, in U.S. Congress, 85th Congress, 1st Session, House of Representatives, Committee Report No. 1125, Aug. 13, 1957.

69   *will be taken.* Brady to Roark, Feb. 18, 1960, PWMC.

69   *federal appropriations for the Memorial.* Christiansen to Albright, Dec. 5, 1960; Gratz to Solomons, Dec. 9, 1960; Albright to Coleman, Dec. 12, 1960; Albert to Gratz, March 17, 1960; Custer to Albert, March 22, 1960; Albert to Custer, May 16, 1960, PWMC. "Ship's Survivors Sought", Oklahoma City *Times*, Feb. 15, 1960, p. 3. Custer to Ballas, Feb. 22, 1960, p. 3, personal files of David McClung.

Congressional Appropriation

70   *appropriation for the construction of the Memorial.* Gratz to Burns, March 6, 1959, PWMC.

70   *"with a jaundiced eye."* Burns to Gratz, May 3, 1959, PWMC.

70   *"go back on my word." ibid.*

70   *"appropriation for construction."* Long to Gratz, July 9, 1960, PWMC.

70   *"neither support nor oppose"* Office of the Secretary of the Navy, Legislative Affairs, to Vinson, undated [1960], PWMC.

70   *"I am a private in your army."* Baker to Gratz, Sept. 21, 1960, PWMC.

70   *"to approve [HR 44]."* Custer to Gratz, July 15, 1961; Russell to Gratz, July 24, 1961, PWMC.

70   *his key committee.* Howard to Custer, Sept. 11, 1961; Custer to Gratz, July 19, 1961, PWMC.

70   *"Hawaii, on December 7, 1941."* United States Public Law 87–201.

71   *"dangers of surprise attack."* U.S. Congress. *Congressional Record,* Vol. 106, Part 11, p. 15064, June 30, 1960; Vol. 107, Part 11, p. 14065, July 31, 1961.

71   *"be caught unprepared." ibid.*

71   *the entombed crewmen.* U.S. Congress. *Congressional Record,* Vol. 107, Part 11, pp.14063–65, July 31, 1961.

Design, Construction, and Dedication

72   *a picnic area.* MacCauley, T.H., "A Watery Grave on the Loose?", undated; Kosco to PWMC, April 24, 1958; Fourteenth Naval District Public Works Office suggestion form, Nov. 10, 1958, PWMC.

72   *no design specifications.* Minutes, Aug. 20, 1959, PWMC. Alfred Preis, interview with author, Honolulu, Aug. 18, 1982.

73   *"plans for the Memorial."* PWMC to Quinn, Nov. 3, 1959, PWMC. Alfred Preis, interview with author, Honolulu, Aug. 18, 1982.

73   *flame on the hulk of the Arizona.* Alfred Preis, interview with author, Honolulu, Aug. 18, 1982.

74   *more than $500,000.* "Highlights—USS Arizona Memorial", undated [1966]; Minutes, June 27, 1960, PWMC.

74   *in time for a December 7 ceremony.* Custer to Wright, Jan. 28, 1960; Custer to Topp, April 4, 1961; PWMC to Hawaii State Dept. of Budget and Review, Aug. 29, 1961; Campbell to Sallet, Nov. 3, 1961, PWMC.

Memorial and remains of USS Utah—the only wreckage from the attack, besides the Arizona, left in Pearl Harbor.

Part IV: 1963–Present

Congress and the Visitor Center

p. 77   *senior Navy and political figures.* Bush to Inouye, Sept. 14, 1967; Mack to Bush, Sept. 12, 1967; Inouye to Burns, Sept. 18, 1967; Burns to Sharp, Sept. 25, 1967, PWMC.

77   *improving the shoreside facility.* AMSFS, III–5. Notes of Jan. 4, 1968 meeting between Lynch and PWMC, PWMC.

77   *a museum and theater complex.* Albright to Hawaii Congressional delegation, undated [1968], PWMC.

77   *for such a bill.* Matsunaga Discussion Draft, undated [1968], PWMC.

77   *strictly Navy Affair.* Minutes, July 28, 1968, PWMC.

78   *"another U.S. agency ... "* CINCPACFLT to CNO, July ? (date illegible), 1968, PWMC.

78   *the Navy's museum system.* Manning to Gratz, July 22, 1968, PWMC.

78   *complex at the shuttle boat landing.* COMFOURTEEN to CNO, Aug. 9, 1968, PWMC.

78   *state of Hawaii.* Bakutis to Matsunaga, Aug. 20, 1968, PWMC.

78   *fundraising for the proposed Visitor Center.* Bakutis to Tobin, Aug. 9, 1968, PWMC.

78   *"at Gettysburg [National Military Park]."* Rivers to Matsunaga, Jan. 28, 1969; Matsunaga to Rivers, Jan. 23, 1969, PWMC.

78   *"funding is recommended."* CNO to COMFOURTEEN, May 15, 1969, PWMC.

78   *"construction of this project."* Ryan to House Armed Services Committee, April 23, 1970, PWMC.

78   *"enactment of House Bill [sic] 206 ... "* Wright to Haward, Sept. 21, 1971, PWMC.

78   *"the wishes of the Pacific War Memorial Commission."* Hayward to Wright, Sept. 23, 1971, PWMC.

79   *sun for waiting visitors.* Matsunaga to Morton, Nov. 2, 1971, PAAR.

79   *"another Federal agency" to operate it.* Matsunaga to Custer, March 21, 1972, PWMC.

80   *"it will be a national park."* U.S. Congress, 92nd Congress, House of Representatives, House Armed Services Full Committee Consideration of HR 16233, HR 14546, HR 16201 . . . , Aug. 9, 1972.

80   *doomed its chances.* Thurmond to Wright, Sept. 13, 1972, PWMC. "Navy Refuses to Aid Arizona Shrine Project", *SB*, March 20, 1972, p. A–1. "House OKs Memorial Expansion", *Adv*, Aug. 17, 1972, p. B–6. U.S. Congress, 92nd Congress, House of Representatives, Committee Report No. 92–1327, Aug. 10, 1972.

80   *"your committee, Mr. Chairman."* U.S. Congress, 92nd Congress, House of Representatives, Transcript of testimony before House Armed Services Subcommittee No. 4, Aug. 2, 1972 (unedited), PAAR.

81   *all Americans who fought in the Pacific Theater.* U.S. Congress, 92nd Congress, House of Representatives, House Armed Services Subcommittee No. 4 Hearings on HR 16201 . . . , March 20, 1972 and Aug. 2, 1972; House Armed Services Full Committee Consideration of HR 16233, HR 14546, HR 16201 . . . , Aug. 9, 1972.

81   *"shore–based personnel and civilians."* ibid.

81   *"guard down at any time ... "* ibid.

82   *"friendship among all nations."* ibid.

82   *"those noble objectives."* ibid.

82   *"Pacific Ocean areas during World War II."* U.S. Congress, 92nd Congress, House of Representatives, HR 16201

82   *"What are we doing?"* U.S. Congress, 92nd Congress, House of Representatives, House Armed Services Committee Hearings on HR 16201 . . . , Aug. 9, 1972.

83   *Arizona Memorial shuttle boats.* Robert Barrel, interview with author, Honolulu, Aug. 6, 1982. U.S. Navy, Fourteenth Naval District, "A Navy Concern for Environment", undated [1971], with cover memo Timberlake to "agency Representatives interested in the 'Kokua' recreational concept–Aiea Bay–Pearl Harbor", Nov. 24, 1971, PAAR.

83   *include the Arizona Memorial.* Hulett to NPS Legislative Counsel, July 31, 1972, PAAR.

83   *the lack of a completed study.* Barrel to Chapman, Oct. 26, 1976, PAAR.

83   *before moving Matsunaga's bills.* U.S. Congress, 92nd Congress, House of Representatives, Transcript of testimony before House Armed Services Subcommittee No. 4, Aug. 2, 1972 (unedited), PAAR.

83   *in southeast Oahu.* Reed to Stennis, Oct. 3, 1972, PAAR.

83   *"considering" Congressional proposals.* Griswold to Chief, NPS Div. of Legislative Coordination and Support, Jan. 22, 1973, and Feb. 21, 1973, PAAR.

83   *"the military construction program."* Willett to Hebert, July 12, 1973, AMSFS, Appendix B–4.

83   *halt the bill's progress.* Matsunaga to Custer, Aug. 9, 1973, PWMC.

At the dedication of the new Memorial, May 30, 1962, marines fired a salute in honor of the dead still entombed within the sunken Arizona.

83   *"burdens and budget restraints."* Griswold to Chief, NPS Div. of Legislation, June 20, 1973, PAAR.

Fourteenth Naval District Study

84   *primarily military mission.* AMSFS, III–30–40.
84   *"her final resting place."* Morgan to Matsunaga, Mar. 1, 1972, AMSFS, Appendix E–3.
84   *"has with the Navy."* Blanchard to COMFOURTEEN, March 27, 1974, filed with AMSFS.
84   *requirements be suitable.* AMSFS, III–30–40.
84   *"the Navy's image." ibid.*
85   *"the new visitor center ... "* COMFOURTEEN to Director, Naval Historical Center, March 24, 1978, filed with AMSFS.

The Arizona Memorial Museum Asociation

86   *money from private donors.* Burns to Nolan, undated [Jan. or Feb. 1974], AMMF.
86   *chartered to lead the drive.* AMMF "Petition for Charter of Incorporation", Jan. 14, 1974, AMMF.
86   *another private nonprofit organization.* AMSFS, III–9. "Navy Ponders Proposals for Pearl Harbor Museum", *SB*, Feb. 28, 1974, p. C–10.
86   *erect its museum building.* PHMM prospectus, PWMC.
86   *"performed by the Pearl Harbor Memorial Museum."* Sessler to Rogers, March 15, 1974, PAAR.
86   *"Pearl Harbor on December 7, 1941."* AMSFS, III–11, V–2, Appendix B–14.
86   *joint plan for the Visitor Center.* "Get It Together", *SB*, May 17, 1974, p. A–18.
86   *"attitudes towards our proposals."* "Private Memorial Fund Drive Backed by Navy", *SB*, June 26, 1974, p. C–7. Minutes, Sept. 17, 1974, AMMF.
87   *state of Hawaii.* "Memorandum of Understanding Between the Department of the Navy and Branch 46 Fleet Reserve Association, Arizona Memorial Museum Foundation", Dec. 19, 1974, AMMF. U.S. Navy, COMNAV-BASE Pearl Harbor, "Pearl Harbor's $5 million Visitors Center", in "Press Kit, 40th Anniversary of the Pearl Harbor Attack", Dec. 7, 1981. Gary Beito, interview with author, Honolulu, June 30, 1982. Hawaii State Legislature, Senate Bill 2208–78, S.D. 1, H.D. 1, C.D. 1 (1978 state budget), p. 79a.
87   *endorse the AMMF campaign.* PWMC to Ariyoshi, undated [1978]; Custer file memo, Feb. 2, 1977, PWMC. Faith Evans, interview with author, Honolulu, Aug. 24, 1982.

Transfer to the National Park Service

88   *funds for the Visitor Center.* Middendorf to Rogers, March 12, 1975, PAAR.
88   *"at appropriate standards."* Lyons to Middendorf, April 11, 1975; Frizzell to Middendorf, Aug. 19, 1975, PAAR.
88   *nor the NPS would support it.* "Interagency Bickering Blocks Visitor Center", *SB*, Dec. 5, 1975, p. A–2. Matsunaga to Custer, July 1, 1976, PWMC.
88   *"a report on this."* File memo, undated [1977] re meeting between Matsunaga and PWMC staff, PWMC.
89   *"completion of such facilities."* File memo, undated [1977] re meeting between Matsunaga and PWMC staff, PWMC. U.S. Congress, 95th Congress, House of Representatives, House Report No. 95–494, "Military Construction Authorization Act Conference Report", July 12, 1977, p. 34.
89   *Vietnam War.* Sen. Daniel Inouye, interview with author, Washington, D.C., May 13, 1983.
90   *between the agencies.* "Letter of Agreement, Arizona Memorial Complex", March 7, 1978/April 21, 1978, PAAR.
90   *for specific purposes.* Bill Loo, interview with author, Pearl Harbor, Aug. 6, 1982.
90   *"requested as soon as possible."* Nystedt to Barrel, May 10, 1977, PAAR.
91   *would be free.* "Use Agreement Arizona Memorial Complex, Naval Station Pearl Harbor, Hawaii" (No. N6274280RP00029), March 21, 1980; "Support Agreement", Sept. 10, 1980, PAAR.

Challenges For the Future

92   *unequal to the demand.* NPS figures.
94   *"is taking place."* Hall, John W., "Pearl Harbor Thirty Years After—Reflections on the Pathology of War and Nationalism", a paper presented at the Fukuoka UNESCO Conference on U.S.–Japanese Relations, Aug. 1971. Quoted in Asada, Sadao, "Japanese Perceptions of the A–Bomb Decision, 1945–1980", in Dixon, Joe C., ed. *The American Military in the Far East: Proceedings of the Ninth Military History Symposium, United States Air Force Academy,* 1–3 October 1980, United States Air Force Academy and Office of Air Force History, Headquarters USAF, 1980, p. 216.

The USS Arizona Memorial and Visitor Center Today

A Popular Destination

The *Arizona* Memorial and shoreside Visitor Center, one of the most heavily visited sites in Hawaii, is also one of the most popular destinations in the U.S. National Park system. Despite the obstacles to its establishment, the complex's annual visitation now tops the one million mark.

Most visitors are U.S. citizens, but the Memorial attracts tens of thousands from Asian nations (including Japan), Europe, Canada, Latin America, and Australia as well. Those who visit the site, just as those who worked to bring the *Arizona* Memorial into existence, are moved by a wide range of emotions and variety of interpretations as to its meaning. But, by their presence, all acknowledge the impact of the Pearl Harbor attack on the course of modern history and ultimately on the lives of countless millions around the world.

At the entrance to the Visitor Center is one of the USS *Arizona'* three anchors, salvaged from the floor of Pearl Harbor after the attack. Weighing 19,585 pounds, the anchor was cast at Chester, Pennsylvania in 1911.

Covering the south side of the Visitor Center lobby is a 50 by 15 foot mural depicting the *Arizona* at sea in the summer of 1941. Painted by marine artist John Roach and commissioned by the Pearl Harbor Survivors Association, it portrays the *Arizona*, escorted by the destroyer *Downes*, steaming off Diamond Head about six months before both ships fell victims to Japanese bombs at Pearl Harbor.

The Visitor Center Museum features photographs and artifacts related to the Pearl Harbor attack. Exhibits deal with the December 7 attack, the battleship *Arizona*, everyday life of the ship's crew, and America's entry into World War II. The displays were designed by exhibit specialists at the National Park Service's interpretive center at Harper's Ferry, West Virginia.

Adjacent to the museum is a bookstore operated by the *Arizona* Memorial Museum Association, a private nonprofit organization. Proceeds from the bookstore help support the National Park Service's interpretive programs at the *Arizona* Memorial. The association offers a wide variety of books on the Pearl Harbor attack, World War II in general, and naval history.

Left: *Nightlighting emphasizes the Memorial's eternal tree of life symbol. "Overtones of sadness have been omitted to permit the individual to contemplate his own personal responses . . . his innermost feelings."*

Alfred Preis, Architect

Below: *View from the "Back Porch", a popular spot behind the Visitor Center.*

Palm trees and fountains grace Visitor Center courtyard.

The courtyard outside the bookstore and museum is divided into three islands by a series of fountains. Each island is planted with Manila Palm trees, and the courtyard perimeter is planted with Family Palms. Between the second and third fountains is a teakwood deck walkway connecting the bookshop-museum area to the theater entrance. The walkway is reminiscent of the teak decks of U.S. Navy battleships such as *Arizona.* From the lawn area west of the courtyard visitors can gaze out over the focal points of the December 7, 1941 attack: Pearl Harbor's East Loch, Ford Island, the *Arizona* Memorial structure and Battleship Row.

The Visitor Center's two air conditioned theaters each seats 151 viewers. There on full size movie screens visitors may watch a 20 minute film that covers *Arizona* history and the Pearl Harbor attack, as well as the background and subsequent course of World War II in the Pacific. Much of the film is authentic footage taken by combat photographers and newsreel camera crews.

The USS *Arizona* Memorial, accessible by shuttle boat from the Visitor Center, lies about one half mile from the shoreside complex. The Memorial resembles a covered bridge spanning the sunken hulk of the USS *Arizona,* lying where she sunk in approximately 40 feet of water. The 184-foot white concrete structure rests on concrete pilings sunk into the floor of the harbor on either side of the sunken ship. No part of the Memorial touches the *Arizona.*

Approached from the water, one of the most noticeable architectural features is a dip in the center of the roofline which rises to peaks at either end of the Memorial. Twenty-one large openings on the sides and roof admit a flood of sunlight into the central portion of the Memorial. Adding to the dramatic effect is the cantilevered design in which the ends of the structure overhang the concrete pilings.

Both sides of the Pearl Harbor story are presented in the Visitor Center museum.

Museum displays and spaces are designed for easy circulation.

The restored World War II submarine, Bowfin, is open to the public by the Pacific Fleet Submarine Memorial Association. It is located within walking distance of the Visitor Center.

Chester W. Nimitz, Admiral and Commander of the Pacific Fleet, at the signing of the surrender of Japan aboard the USS Missouri on September 2, 1945.

After disembarking at the *Arizona* Memorial's landing, visitors climb a short flight of stairs to the entrance area. There they see the original ship's bell from the *Arizona*. Once past the bell, the main assembly area offers dramatic views of the sunken ship. The main decks lie just below the surface of the water and are plainly visible. At low tide many of the coamings and bulkhead remains are awash. To the immediate left lies the forward part of the *Arizona*, with the galley area clearly visible. Further forward the remains of the number two gun turret can be seen. Just to the right of the Memorial is a flagstaff attached to the base of the ship's main mast. Beyond the flagstaff the foundation of the number three gun turret rises from the water. One of the most sobering features of the wreckage is the thin film of fuel oil which continually seeps from the hulk in the vicinity of the number three turret foundation.

At the end of the assembly area is a viewing well which allows visitors to look down on the *Arizona's* starboard side. On ceremonial occasions flowers are cast on the water through this opening. The well affords a view of the curved splinter shields for the 1.1 inch antiaircraft guns which were scheduled for installation but had not yet been mounted when the ship was sunk.

Past the viewing well is the shrine room. Window-like cutout designs on either side of this room represent the eternal tree of life. At the end of the room is a marble wall on which are inscribed the name and rank of each of the 1,177 who perished aboard the *Arizona*. These silent ranks of names truly represent the ultimate consequences of war, and it is here more than anyplace else in the Memorial complex that we are forced to ponder the meaning of the *Arizona* Memorial.

The flagstaff which seems to be a part of the Memorial structure is actually mounted on the sunken Battleship Arizona.

Boat ride to the Memorial is preceded by a film in one of the Visitor Center's two theaters. (top) Twin–screw, 150–passenger boats operated by Navy crews shuttle visitors to the Memorial. (above) The "Back Porch" is a favorite place for a view. (right)

The Memorial's main deck with shrine room
in the background. (top) Clearly visible
from the Memorial is the Arizona's remains,
(left) still seeping fuel oil. (above)

Visitor Center seen from the air. Landfill during the World War II construction boom created this area from a tidal marsh.

USS Arizona Memorial Visitor Center

1 Anchor
2 Entrance
3 Bookstore
4 Museum
5 Twin Theaters
6 Boat Landing
7 Lanai ("Back Porch")
8 Administrative Offices
9 Courtyard & Fountains
10 Snack Shop

The Memorial and Visitor Center are open every day of the year except Mondays, Thanksgiving, Christmas, and New Year's Day. The first tour of the day begins about 8am, and the last one starts at 3pm. If you need additional information to plan your visit, please contact:

The Superintendent
USS Arizona Memorial
1 Arizona Memorial Place
Honolulu, HI 96818

For recorded information phone:
(808) 422-0561

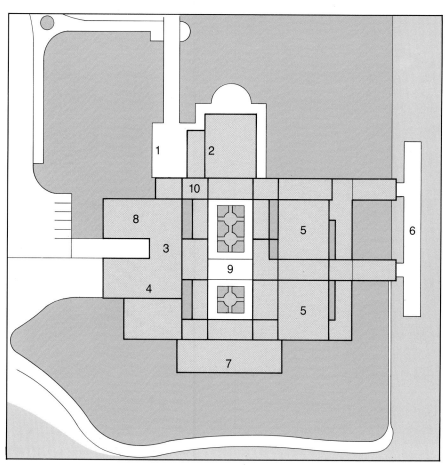